I'M THE ONE

THAT KNOW

THIS COUNTRY!

Kulinma Wiya tjuta kutjupa tjutanti nyiri nyang ka ngaranyi. Ka nyura nyiri nyangatja alara nyakulan ngalturingkuku munu kuntaringkutu.

Readers of this work should be aware that if members of some Aboriginal communities see names or images of the deceased, particularly their relatives, they may be distressed. Before using this work in such communities, readers should establish the wishes of senior members and take their advice on appropriate procedures and safeguards to be adopted.

I'M THE ONE THAT KNOW THIS COUNTRY!

by Jessie Lennon

Aboriginal Studies Press

First published in 2000
by Aboriginal Studies Press
Second edition published in 2011 by Aboriginal Studies Press

© Main text: Jessie Lennon 2011, held by Emily Betts (nee Lennon) for the Lennon family.
© Caption material: Michele Madigan and Anne Johnson 2011.
Individual essay © Maggie Brady 2011.
All images reproduced with the permission of the copyright holders.

All rights reserved. No part of this book may be reproduced or transmitted in any form or by any means, electronic or mechanical, including photocopying, recording or by any information storage and retrieval system, without prior permission in writing from the publisher. The Australian *Copyright Act 1968* (the Act) allows a maximum of one chapter or 10 per cent of this book, whichever is the greater, to be photocopied by any educational institution for its education purposes, provided that the educational institution (or body that administers it) has given a remuneration notice to Copyright Agency Limited (CAL) under the Act.

Aboriginal Studies Press
is the publishing arm of the
Australian Institute of Aboriginal
and Torres Strait Islander Studies
GPO Box 553, Canberra, ACT 2601
Phone: (61 2) 6246 1183
Fax: (61 2) 6261 4288
Email: asp@aiatsis.gov.au
Web: www.aiatsis.gov.au/asp/about.html

National Library of Australia
Cataloguing-In-Publication data:

  Author: Lennon, Jessie, 1925–1998

  Title: I'm the one that know this country / Jessie Lennon.

  Edition: Revised ed.

  ISBN: 9780855757199 (pbk.)

  Notes: Includes bibliographical references.

  Subjects: Lennon, Jessie, 1925-
  Women, Aboriginal Australian — South Australia — Coober Pedy Region — Biography. Coober Pedy (S. Aust.) — History.

  Dewey Number: 305.89915094238

Compiled and edited by Michele Madigan
Additional material by Anne Johnson, Coober Pedy Historical Society

Printed in Australia by Bluestar Print

Contents

Notes on language, Pronunciation, Abbreviations	vi
Acknowledgments	viii
Map	ix
Introduction	xi
Prologue	xv

Chapter 1
Kingoonya: Early life — 1

Chapter 2
The Travelling: Learning from the Old People — 22

Chapter 3
Coober Pedy: 'I grow up here' — 30

Chapter 4
Epic journey: 'That's our honeymoon trip' — 52

Chapter 5
Settling down: Going for opal — 64

Chapter 6
Displaced: 'The bomb caught us' — 88

Chapter 7
Drifting: 'Everything went funny then' — 104

Chapter 8
Going home: 'I got sick over the bomb' — 120

Chapter 9
Last word: 'I'm the one who know' — 140

Epilogue	143
The Long-lasting Legacy of Maralinga *Maggie Brady*	145
Timeline	154
References	157

Notes on language

Re Matutjara / Antikirinya / Yankunyjatjara: Some translations in the body of the text are free translations of the Western Desert languages, not literal ones.

Re Aboriginal English as a recognised language: *Aboriginal English has been maintained as a distinct variety of English because it is particularly suited to embodying what Indigenous people want to say to one another, in an Indigenous context, adapting and using English to express an Indigenous world view. As a result Aboriginal English is integrally related to the identity and culture of Indigenous people.* From *Language and Communication Enhancement for Two-way Education*, Ian G. Malcolm, 1995.

Re usage and construction:

In Aboriginal English, 'been' is an indicator of past tense, for example, 'he been say'; 'I been tell him'.

Plural marking using 's' is a feature of English grammer often used when words from Aboriginal languages are used in English, for example *tjilpis*.

A common construction in Aboriginal languages is an extension sentence: several additions to the end of a particular sentence. Note how frequently Jessie Lennon transfers this device to Aboriginal English by way of explaining something in more detail. For example, *they seen how they used to travel, those old time people, old tjilpis — old whitefellas looking around — those swaggies, their swag on an old wheel ...* (p.11).

Pronunciation guide

Stress the first syllable in all words
u is pronounced as in *put*
a is pronounced as in *pass*, but is 'shorter'
i is pronounced as in *pin*
tj is a single sound made by putting the tongue behind the top teeth.
ny is a single sound, like the first sound in *news*
ng is single sound, as in the final sound in *sing*
p, t and k often sound like English b, d and g. There is no aspiration puff of air as in English p, t, k (word beginnings)
otherwise consonants k, l, m, n, p, t, w and y are pronounced as you would in English
r is flapped or rolled as in Scottish English
r̲ is like an American 'r' as in *farm* (tongue tipped back)
pronounce l̲, n̲, t̲, as if there was an 'r' in front — rl, rn, rt

Abbreviations

AIATSIS	Australian Institute of Aboriginal and Torres Strait Islander Studies
DOSAA	Division of State Aboriginal Affairs (South Australia)
CPHS	Coober Pedy Historical Society
NAA	National Archives of Australia
NLA	National Library of Australia
PIRSA	Primary Industries and Resources, South Australia
SAM	South Australian Museum
UAM	United Aborigines Mission

Dedicated to a loving Mum, Grandmother and Unta (Great-grandmother)

JESSIE LENNON

It came as a surprise to us when she had her first book. Now this is her second book. She had a lot of stories and she'd tell them to us in her own style; she'd tell them to you the way she lived her own life, that same way, just that simple Aboriginal way. *Emily Betts (nee Lennon)*

Acknowledgments

I'm the one that know this country! is the initiative and work of Jessie Lennon. In 1993, she asked Michele Madigan to 'help me make my book'. For the first two-and-a-half years of this project we had the wonderful support and encouragement of the late Ricky Brown. Our thanks to him, and thanks also to Eileen Wani Wingfield, to Beaver Lennon and to Emily Betts for their later help with the manuscript.

Thanks to Joan Healy and Elizabeth Manusutti for encouragement to persevere with this longer text of Jessie's story after the publication of *And I Always Been Moving! The early life of Jessie Lennon.* Thanks also to Max Jones.

We are grateful to Anne Johnson for her generous work on the Coober Pedy photographs and captions that support Jessie's story. We also thank the members of the Coober Pedy Historical Society who, through Anne, generously made available to us many wonderful photographs they hold; a number now published for the first time in this book. Thanks to the individual copyright holders from all over Australia for kindly sharing photographs: in particular Mrs Ivy McWilliams, Joe Kennedy and Mrs Rhonda Traeger. Also to those working in institutions which supplied photographs, in particular Kate Alport of the South Australian Museum and Carole Cooper and David Jeffrey of AIATSIS.

Thanks to Christobel Mattingley for her personal support. As well, tribute is paid to the work of Christobel, her co-editor Ken Hampton, the Aboriginal contributors and the Council associated with the superb book *Survival in Our Own Land* (1988). Readers will find this classic reference to Nunga and Anangu experience in South Australia quoted in the captions a number of times. Thanks to Umoona Community Council Inc. for permission to use the excellent map. Thanks also to other people listed in the bibliography who shared information used in the captions.

Acknowledgment and thanks to the Sisters of St Joseph Aboriginal Ministry Fund, Sydney, for the essential initial funding of this project.

Finally, thanks to Christel Hauri, Christine Schwerdt, Cheryle Thomson, Margaret Kenny, Andrea Dean, Lorraine Gatehouse and Joe Golemac for their practical support.

Extracts from *I'm the one that know this country!* were originally published in *And I Always Been Moving!* They are reproduced here with permission.

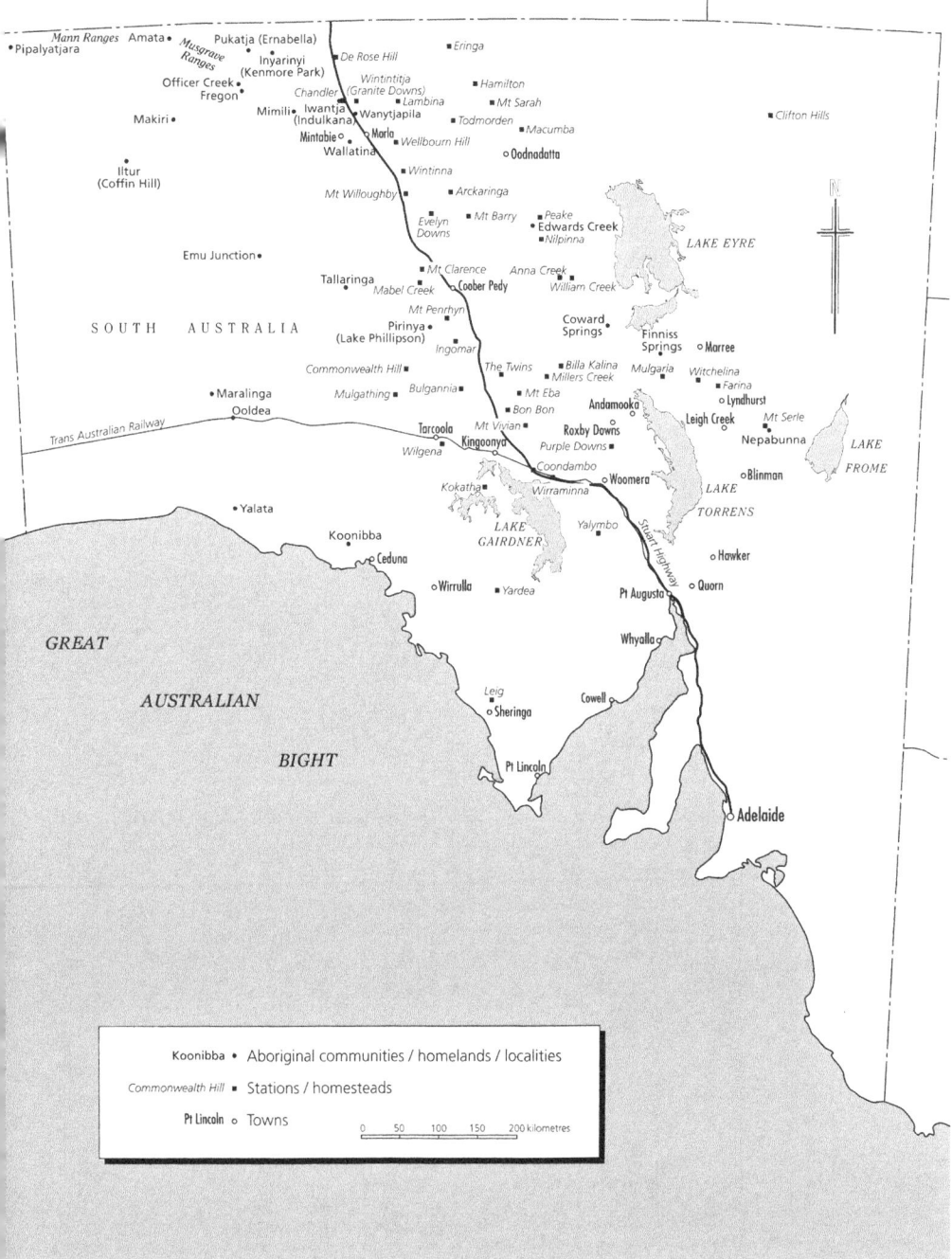

South Australian pastoral stations, towns and Aboriginal communities and localities. Reproduced with permission of Umoona Community Council Inc, Coober Pedy.

Introduction

Jessie Lennon, a Ma_tutjara woman of the Australian Western Desert, was born on a sheep station near Kingoonya in the 1920s. For much of her long life she was 'always moving' — travelling, living and working in the vast desert regions of South Australia. This was her country, and she knew it intimately from a young age.

On foot, on camels and sometimes 'jumping the train', Jessie and her family often travelled hundreds of kilometres at a time, through the driest, driest country in which A_nangu (Aboriginal people) have survived for tens of thousands of years.

Jessie's journeys began at about the age of six, when she accompanied her father Nylatu, a traditional man, on a ceremonial journey with the Old People, senior A_nangu. The Travelling took them from Kingoonya as far west as Ooldea in the time of the famed Daisy Bates and as far north as Coober Pedy, then in its infancy as an opal mining settlement.

Later she moved with her mother Kutin (Rosie) and stepfather Billy Austin as they sought 'whitefella' work in towns, on sheep and cattle stations, and on the Netting (the famous Dog Fence). Then, as a young bride, Jessie and her husband Barney Lennon embarked on an epic honeymoon journey throughout the central eastern area of the state, to unfamilar country. Their return home involved, among other things, a hazardous adventure clinging to a fast goods train.

On many occasions, Jessie's travels brought her back to Coober Pedy (today a thriving mining and tourism town). Here she had her first child, lived in camps, underground dugouts or out on the fields, and worked alongside her family 'noodling' on the mine dumps for precious opal scraps from which they could earn a living. Her later years were spent in Coober Pedy and some of her family still live there.

In the 1950s, while living in the Coober Pedy area, Jessie and her family were 'caught by the bomb' — fallout from the British nuclear tests at Emu, north of Maralinga, which came through Mabel Creek Station and drifted on to Twelve Mile opal field. The people were not evacuated, nor advised to take any precautions. Jessie and her family fled to the east, but they did not escape the long-term effects on their health. These emerged some decades later and led Jessie, by then a great-grandmother and respected senior woman in the community, to take up the as yet unsuccessful fight for compensation.

A natural storyteller, Jessie Lennon recounts her life's journeys in her own words. As a Matutjara woman, she spoke the dialect of her mother, similar to other closely related dialects of Antikirinya and Yankunytjatjara, and also to Pitjantjatjara, all variations of the widespread Western Desert language. With whitefellas she spoke Aboriginal English. In this book she speaks both.

Her words are subtle, and her telling of events understated; compelling us to travel with her at a leisurely pace, taking time to absorb the significance of her stories. If we do so, we gain an Anangu perspective, not only of daily life in the desert and the extraordinary adaptations the people were forced to make, but also of some significant developments in settler history — the growth of the pastoral industry and mining, the construction of railway lines and highways.

Through Jessie's telling of her mother's 'long-ago stories', we gain insight into Anangu's experiences of first contact with Europeans, and the changes that the expansion of transport brought to the area's traditional people, for example the demise of a traditional meeting place at Ooldea Soak. We also see well-known sheep and cattle stations such as at Wilgena, Bon Bon, Twinsfield and Roxby Downs through the experiences of Aboriginal stationhands — so long the backbone of the pastoral industry. We learn too of life, food and work for Anangu at missions such as Ooldea, Umeewarra and Finnis Springs.

Jessie's stories are juxtaposed with historic photographs and background information relating to the times, places and people of her life. These not only provide context, but act as something of a potted social history of South Australian settlements such as Coober Pedy, Kingoonya, Tarcoola, Andamooka and Ceduna — places whose stories are themselves tapestries of tough, colourful characters, of boom times and bust, in an unforgiving climate and landscape.

As much as Jessie's life is full of journeys, so is it of homecomings, and through these emerge a vivid picture of her family life, and of the importance of 'home'. She is indeed the 'one that know this country', and loved it.

Jessie took great pride and pleasure in preparing the manuscript for this book. As it neared completion, and despite ill health, she came alive during sessions with Michele Madigan — revising earlier drafts, checking everything, adding incidents and details, enjoying reliving her eventful life. The book fulfils Jessie's wish that her stories, in her own words, be published for her children, grandchildren and great-grandchildren. But she also 'made the book' for us all, especially 'the latecomers' who 'don't yet know these things' ... that we might learn.

Introduction

The Company's Patch
Aboriginal people walked this area for tens of thousands of years. European explorer John McDouall Stuart passed through in 1858, but opal as gemstone was not discovered here until 1915. This led to a very productive mining industry and the development of the town of Coober Pedy. The original opal find was made by 14-year-old Will Hutchison, from a small gold prospecting party led by his father. This photograph is of the first opal mine, called The Company's Patch, five kilometres south-west of Coober Pedy. According to opal historian Kath Crilly, it was taken in October 1916 by the South Australian Director of Mines, who was making the first official inspection of the opal discovery. *Photograph: PIRSA; CPHS*

Vic Williamson's dugout
This early dugout was once occupied by long-time miner Vic Williamson, a very strong and respected Swede who was known for his willingness to advise newcomers. Where the dugout was is now Radeka's underground accommodation, in central Coober Pedy. *Photograph: Murray Chambers; CPHS*

I'm the one that know this country!

Wilgena Station
Wilgena Station, first taken up in the nineteenth century, remains as a pastoral lease with the McBride family today. In this family group, photographed at Wilgena in 1925, it is thought that the man with the beard may be Jessie Lennon's father, Nylatu. *Photograph: T.B. Robertson; SAM Anthropology Archives*

Prologue

Coober Pedy, it's all built up now — no space in it at all. I can't see it in the same way — nothing. All the dugouts in the front. Everywhere I move my head, I see dugouts. I don't see that space where I've been playing around and looking at the trees there — green down in there and the shop down there where the garage is — old Vic Williamson, that shopkeeper's dugout ...

Everything wasn't started here like the offices and all that you know — where people getting jobs and all that. There was nothing, no shops here. Just a store and lately they're getting all this.

And I can put it down here in a book and they believe that? That's the one thing — I'm the first one eh? All the women folk have a meeting and they say, 'Who the people been here longest?' (been long enough — like that). 'Who the people, the first one that came here?'

Ngayulu wangkanyi kulintjaku — I'm talking like this so people will understand. A lot of times somebody is trying to be more than what I know. They think they know more here ...

... But we fellas, we came from Kingoonya to here, travelling on camels. We're the people that have been here longer. I'm an old woman now and I don't care what I say 'cause I been **here**, I grew up **here!**

I started when I was a little girl from here. Little girl — mother brought us — me, my brothers — here. (Some of my brothers went home to God and I'm the one sister left.)

And our children — when I had Bernard, Emily, Beaver, Stanley — and Joe was nothing — oh, we sat down for a long time with the kids over here, Coober Pedy.

I'm the one who know everyway — *Ngura nyangatja ngayuku*. This is my home.

I'm the one that know this country!

Wilgena Station — 1925 anthropological expedition
In November 1925, around the time of Jessie Lennon's birth, T.B. Robertson and others from the South Australian Museum made an anthropological expedition to Wilgena Station to study the characteristics of the Aboriginal people living there. As was the practice of the time, the people were divided into blood groups, their measurements were taken and observations were made, sometimes intrusively, of their physical characteristics. Notes and photographs, such as this, were taken to document observations of their way of life.
Photograph: T.B. Robertson; SAM Anthropology Archives

CHAPTER 1
Kingoonya: Early life

Wilgena

I born Wilgena. See, I want to say this. I grewed up there — mother had me there, baby. Carried me round there — grew me up. My sister was born there too.

After that we came back to Kingoonya. We always go where they want — mother, stepfather.

'We'll go back to Wilgena working, shearing sheep.' We'll go back to the place where I was born.

Two fathers

By now, my mother went with the second man — that old fella married to her too. He's my stepfather, Willie Austin's father. He grew me up, he looked after me there at Kingoonya.

They had an argument those two mens (my father and Willie Austin's father). I don't know, I think my stepfather was my Dad. That's all I know. When I grew up I find out who my father was. I call the two of them Dad.

They liked one another then.

I'm the one that know this country!

Kingoonya

We stopped there — Kingoonya and mother looked after me there. Yes, Kingoonya and my brother, Willie Austin, born in Kingoonya there.

Kingoonya — railway workers houses — for the ones that worked on the line — some houses there. Big shop there. And there was one pub too. And the dance hall there too.

East–West train coming to Kingoonya and some of the ladies would be feeding their children. People on the train would see the babies and children there standing. Call them over and give 'em lollies, apples and oranges.

The Tea and Sugar train would come past too all the time. We sit around on boxes of fruit, some of meat, bread.

Yes, Kingoonya! It's always been our home — our *ngura*. It should be our town, you know. That's where we've been — walkabout, sort of, walking around the country there.

We know the places.

1. Kingoonya: Early life

Kingoonya
'Kingoonya was the great meeting place of the Australian Aborigines,' recounts Frank Berkery in his 1944 publication *East Goes West* about his travels across the East–West line. 'Here the blacks would assemble in full force, their war-like accoutrements a wonderful sight from a safe distance. The surroundings are most effective, the stage setting being formed by the desert bush, with the great desert fresh-water wells in the background.' The township of Kingoonya, 750 kilometres north-west of Adelaide, grew up as a supply centre for the surrounding sheep stations. Characterised by a main street 400 metres wide, 'with many houses in a compact row', it was an important stop, along both the East–West line and the Stuart Highway, and Aboriginal people often sold artefacts to passing travellers.
Photograph: Joe Kennedy; CPHS

Mother's long ago stories

Seeing the whitefellas

And another lot of country again — ''nother side country', Mum said. She was born 'nother side — Tallaringa, Tjalyiri. Mum, Grandmother and Grandfather and uncles all travelling around there. All big mob — a big mob of people came from that way — north.

A long time ago, Mum said, some men came through — *walypalas* — whitefellas. I don't know what for but one man reckon they looking for something. Some minerals, I suppose.

And long time again, before the line, before the railway line went through, they seen how they used to travel, those old time people, old *tjilpis* — old whitefellas looking around — those swaggies, their swag on an old wheel, a pushbike wheel and making a buggy out of and push it along. And they done that again on the railway line. And put the swag, water, flour and things and just camp half-way, I suppose.

I don't know how long they travelled — to Kalgoorlie I suppose.

The workers just put that line there, laying it out. And big lamps there for the workers laying the line.

Mimi Nyung

One place, other side of Kingoonya, called 'Mimi Nyung' — *mimi*, breast — cut off. Somebody must have cut the breast off, named like that. Must have been a Dreaming place. *Ngura ini* — that was the name of the place. They gone into that Mimi Nyung — all the whitefellas. They named it Barton — Barton Siding.

Some women — white girls, older girls — cooked sometimes for them there, for those who were putting the lines through. And *kungkas* (Anangu women) been getting clothes, you know, from these white womans.

And *'tjarpa!'* they been saying to each other, 'put it on!'

And say, 'I got one too!'

Pleased! Happy! Like that! Not standing *nikiti* — naked.

1. Kingoonya: Early life

The East–West (Transcontinental) line
The state of Western Australia was the prime mover in the push to establish the East–West railway line. The new Commonwealth Government finally began the surveying of the route in 1909 only after Western Australia had threatened to secede from the Federation. Work began in 1912. As there were no towns along the route, it was a huge undertaking — everything and everybody required for construction had to brought in. Finding water was a real difficulty and one of the unfortunate side-effects of the railway was the later demise of the Ooldea Soak. Up until 1923 this 'had never failed' the desert people. During construction, camel trains brought 45,000 litres across the sandhills to the line each day. The line was joined on 17 October 1917 between Ooldea (pictured) and Watson sidings, where a sign still marks the spot. *Photograph: Couper-Black; SAM*

I'm the one that know this country!

My father meets the whitefellas

A<u>n</u>angu — Aboriginal people — they were frightened before, like with the white people's faces. And white people, they been trying to get my father. My father, Nylatu, he been run into this whitefella before. He had a cart and a horse and he been sing out. He been sing out, this man, he been sing out to my father. 'Oh pannikin, you know,' he holded up his pannikin, drinking it, showing it to him.

But my father, he been run away! I suppose he been thinking, '*Nyaa palatja?* — what's this?' White, you know — might be a ghost!

Uwa — yes, Mum been telling me a lot of things like that. They been *ngu<u>l</u>u* again — get frightened.

But now, people like A<u>n</u>angu, Mum been say. And people quietened down, you know again with the white people. They knew one another then.

'*Mai panya ngaringu* — food was there,' people would say. 'Come along and get *mai* — get the food.'

Oh, they get used to it then.

1. Kingoonya: Early life

Traditional life meets the newcomers — late 1920s
This photograph, taken not long after Jessie Lennon's birth, highlights the fact that first contact stories, such as those told to Jessie by her mother, still exist well within living memory in northern and western South Australia today. Jessie's father, Nylatu, coming from the north-west, was renamed Archie Nylatu by the newcomers, while her mother, born Kutin in Tjalyiri (or Tallaringa) to the west of what is now Coober Pedy, became Rosie, and later Rosie Austin.

Using a stick spindle, the women would spin the wool from animal fur into a 'string' to make the material for their covering; their needle being a sharpened stick. The wooden bowls or *wira*, still made by hand today and decorated for the tourist trade, were used to carry bush tucker or water and the women would walk long distances in this fashion.
Photograph: Faith Thomas; AIATSIS

North Well

Then we come to North Well. We know the Bosses. Old Mr McBride, he's the owner, Jack Pick the manager. And my mother and father — old stepfather — stopped there more. North Well, this side of Kingoonya — the shearers come, all the shearers shearing sheep.

And the Cookie there, he's got no time — he's the cook and they give Mum a job too — wash clothes, hang it out, like that, working there. And they pay her money too, tucker money, food for us.

And we get cakes — they give cakes to us, a tray full of cake — bread and all what he made.

And we kids think that's a Christmas man!

Looking for rabbit

And sometimes when we've got spare time, we go — Mum take us for walk then. Anyway look for rabbit. Mum like rabbit. '*Nganana yananyi rapitaku* — We'll go looking for rabbit.'

I had my two brothers, Willie and Bobby. Willie having a *tjupu* — piggy-back — on his mother, sitting along. And we two, me and Bob walking — walking behind our Mum.

Anyway look for rabbit.

1. Kingoonya: Early life

Bush tucker — going out for game

Bush tucker, particularly *kuka*, game, still means real food to many Aboriginal people. *Malu*, the kangaroo, remains the prize in the Western Desert area, which includes Coober Pedy. However, the culling practices of the mainstream society, which may mean a trip of a hundred kilometres to find the game, have put it out of the reach of many. *Kalaya*, the emu, is also a preferred meat; traditionally hunted by the men along with the *kipara*, bush turkey.

As this 1995 photograph of Pingkai Lester and her husband Kantji shows, goanna and the *ngintaka*, perentie lizard, may also be caught by women. Further south the wombat is sought after as *kuka*; and women and children go out for *kalta*, sleepy lizard. Until its recent demise, the introduced rabbit was a great staple, being plentiful and easily caught by women and children. It was cooked in a similar manner to the bigger game — thrown on the early fire to singe the fur then placed in the underground natural oven to make a delicious meal. *Photograph: Michele Madigan, reproduced with kind permission of Eileen Kampakuta Brown and Yami Lester (1999)*

Going to Ooldea — and Daisy Bates

We knew then, we knew that country, that sidings and stations. Old father been take us then, **my** old father, old Nylatu. We went to Ooldea and that's the last we went. *Nganana yanu* — we went! My big sister, Molly Brown and Linda Austin (Mungeranie) or Wantjiyla, her Anangu name, again; and Edna Williams' old mother and father — Bamilya and Mickey Fatt.

Caught the train to Ooldea. Jump on, might be Barton — jump on anyway. Clever kids! (Anyway we **think** we're clever when we jump on, jump on the trucks.) Our lot on the train and two trains come together and passing we see one another. Big mob on the other train and call out, 'Oh.........' while the train going past the other way ...

'Oh......' We think that it's wonderful!

But we kids frightened for the guard — hid! And Edna Williams' mother knew and she was watching us all the way.

We went to Ooldea — *Yultu-kutu*. Yes, that's the Anangus' *wangka*, the Aboriginal way to say it again. We went to Ooldea and we was going to Daisy Bates. Daisy was half way down the siding. I don't know how she went there or came but she was camping there all the time: she was stopped there. She got a tent, three tents I think. A lot of girls follow up, watch it there. Oh, there she give 'em *mai* — food, too. They don't call her Daisy Bates.

'Oh *Kaparli*!' they say. '*Kaparli uwa-ni* — Grandmother, give me food!'

I been thinking *Kaparli*? ...

1. Kingoonya: Early life

Daisy Bates
One of the best-known historical figures in Australia was Irish-born Daisy Bates. After living among Aboriginal people in Western Australia, Daisy Bates settled at Ooldea between the soak and the siding in September 1919. Ooldea Soak had always been a traditional gathering place for many related Aboriginal groups. Some of the A̱nangu had begun to stay there longer. Lacking any government support (despite her many pleas), Daisy Bates provided food, clothing and basic medical treatment, funded at first by the sale of her Western Australian property and then by her frequent writings about the people — not all accurate. Unfortunately, the children of mixed relationships were 'always running and hiding from Dais' Bates' in fear of being sent away'. In other respects the people, some of whom are still alive today at Oak Valley and Yalata, appreciated her presence. Life at Ooldea changed with the coming of the missionaries in 1933 and Daisy Bates left Ooldea on Jubilee Day 1936. She spent many years writing and living in a tent at Pyap on the River Murray. From 1941–1945 Daisy Bates moved back to the East-West line, this time to Wynbring. She died in Adelaide in 1951, aged 90. *Photograph: Ernestine Hill; J.D. Hill; NLA*

The strangers coming in

The camp was there, we was stopping there — People, Old People there. And we see all those strangers, coming along. Those Antikirinya mob and Pitjantjatjara was just travelling, just travelling a long way and they came to see that sandhill ... Naked, *nikiti* — no clothes on, *kapi-ku* — they were going for that water, they were going for that soak — Yultu, Ooldea. They were going there — right into there. The Pitjantjatjaras was just travelling. A long way just travelling. Long way they came, just to see that sandhill and that soak.

That's how they lived.

My family, they came from the north down, you know. Later on, they learned the *mai* — the whitefellas' food. But before, they didn't know they were going to run into a line, run into that railway line you know, and run into whitefellas and all. They talk about that. They have a yarn. '*Uwa, wati piran* — yes, whitefella, *wati* — white one.'

Mum was telling me about all this. Eileen Wingfield's mother too. Yes we knew all that — all the Pitjantjatjara there at Ooldea before the mission there. Antikirinya mob mixed up there too with the Pitjantjatjaras. (And still here at Coober Pedy, they're mixed up again.)

Yes, we knew that — Mum, Eileen Wingfield and her mother too knew that — all the Pitjantjatjara mob were there — Ooldea.

1. Kingoonya: Early life

The strangers coming in
In the early 1920s, A.G. Bolam, station master at Ooldea, wrote in *The Trans-Australian Wonderland*:

> The natives seen at Ooldea offer a most interesting study as Ooldea is one of the very few places in Australia where wild blacks from the innermost parts come into contact with civilisation. Blacks ... have, from time immemorial, come into Ooldea for the religious ceremonials ... and to exchange articles. Many of these blacks — men, women and children — never saw a white man until they reached Ooldea; and, of course, on their arrival in camp they were dressed in nature's clothing ... See these wild blacks as they come in from the ranges, in the pink of condition, after their trip of nearly 300 miles, their skins shining with the glow of health, their carriage graceful, their movements machine-like.
>
> They are wonderful men in the bush ... Their knowledge of the habits of animals astounding ... their power of endurance is extraordinary; their sense of humour is unimpeachable. (Quoted from 7th edition, 1930.) *Photograph: H.E. Green, UAM; SAM*

I'm the one that know this country!

Rations at Ooldea Mission

Then ration time came — we go for ration time there. And we were learning, sort of, by going there to Ooldea and we get a little *mai* — food. We see what sort of tucker they been giving us; *mai ulu* — wheat grinded up.

Fill wheat up in the fruit tin, old fruit tin, empty one — that's all. Drop a little sugar in and we there, me and Edna getting it out with our *mara*, with our hand — yes, with our fat little hands.

Uwa! Yes! And I been taste 'em.

And I been thinking, '*Mai wiya nyangatja kulini!* Hey, this isn't food! *Mai tjulpuku!* — This is wheat for chooks!'

1. Kingoonya: Early life

The establishment of Ooldea Mission
In response to the urgent suggestion of the Tarcoola missionary to the United Aborigines Mission (UAM), Miss Annie Lock made an inspection of Ooldea. The UAM accepted her report and in July 1933, she travelled, mostly by horse and trap, 800 kilometres to Ooldea. The ration station was moved from Tarcoola to Ooldea Mission. An iron hut and brush sheds were erected as mission buildings from material left by the railways in the soak area.

As Mrs Alice Mangkatina Cox describes, 'Some A̱nangu began to stay longer at the soak, especially in the drought years. Some of us never went back to the "spinifex". We stayed at the mission or camp.'

Understandably, there was friction between Miss Lock and Daisy Bates a couple of miles away — two women with very different world views. *Photograph courtesy of H.E. Green, UAM; AIATSIS*

I'm the one that know this country!

Ooldea School

The school started there — the Mission school — there at the soak. Just the bush shed, the green bushes cut off from the tree and they built them on to the sheds.

Yes, just sitting on the ground and that fella, that school teacher mark 'em off drawing a line on the ground.

'That's your class, childrens!'

And that 'nother one, 'nother line again — 'Yours!'

Behind that class, we're sitting frontway for a little while, me and Edna Williams with Martha Edwards. We know it all.

And I'm the only one walking around here, Coober Pedy, me and Edna, we're the only ones that seen that school at Ooldea.

1. Kingoonya: Early life

Ooldea Mission and school
After a year alone at the soak, Miss Lock was joined by Miss Tyler who began 'a school in the sand' for five children. Later a brush shed was built. Criticisms continued to be made of Aboriginal people 'frequenting the line'. Reverend J. Sexton was sent on inspection to Ooldea. As a result of his report approving of their trading artefacts at the train, the Government also (in 1938), transferred 5200 square kilometres including Ooldea Soak through the South Australian Government 'for the use of the aborigines'. This also gave the mission security.

Harry Green (pictured) and Marion Green arrived in April 1936 and stayed with the help of various other staff, until the mission closed in June 1952, 'Mr Green's time'. In 1939 they reported the 'extensive building programme' completed, including the school and church and a wireless service to the Kalgoorlie Aerial Medical Base, 960 kilometres away. The Children's Home and a hospital followed. Some of the senior men and women who live at Yalata and Oak Valley today lived at Ooldea at this time, in the home or at the camp.
Photograph: H.E. Green, UAM; AIATSIS

Travelling and jumping the train

Oh yes, we do that — pack up and get on the train and go there, Ooldea. Oh *yannga yananyi* — going on a trip away. Big Travelling there — Travelling. Yes, that's what they was all the time doing.

(And **our** people don't like to be Travelling all the time — young fellas, you know, some of them. '*Wiya* — No, I've got to **work!** I can't be running up and down there.' Like that they were talking.)

Or some might be want to go again. Go a long time. They ready to go — **travel**, go on the train. They can jump on the carriage. They let them if they have the money.

But A<u>n</u>angu, Aboriginal people, go on the goods truck. Sometimes the guard chuck off A<u>n</u>angu there — chuck him off. Spears and boomerangs, pannikin and bag and blankets — **out!**

'I **told** you not to get on the truck anymore!'

But sometimes they were good guards and we fellas get a ride from Ooldea again.

1. Kingoonya: Early life

Travelling
The camps at Ooldea moved frequently, usually at some distance from the mission buildings. Mr Green's 1944 photograph shows how the *kanku's* tarpaulin cover had replaced the leafy boughs. As Ooldea remained an important gathering place for cultural purposes, including marriage arrangements, large groups of Aboriginal visitors continued to arrive at the soak. Many came from the 'spinifex', others were from Tarcoola and Coober Pedy and Cundalee in Western Australia. Up until the 1960s, people continued to walk extraordinary distances to keep up their cultural obligations. Where possible they also took advantage of the new culture, travelling en masse 'jumping the train'. The UAM continued to complain to the Commonwealth Railways about the railway's policies, including their refusal to permit Aboriginal passengers on the East–West express even with a ticket. They had to use the slow, twice weekly 'Tea and Sugar train'. Things changed after a state-wide outcry in 1949 when 100 people travelling to Quorn to feature in the film *Bitter Springs* were forced to travel in the cattle vans, despite having paid £300 for tickets. *Photograph: H.E. Green, UAM; AIATSIS*

Tarcoola — learning whitefella work

They brought us back to Tarcoola again, we fella kids. They'd showed us Yultu — Ooldea. Didn't go that way again then. Came back to Tarcoola again; our father, Old Nylatu, brought us back there. Sitting around there for a long time.

I went there to the old man's station there too — old Bill Roberts, they called him. He's the station owner, you know, and he'd look after anybody — rations. He'd give them *mai* — food. Got fellas there working — old *tjilpis*, old men like fellas that can ride horses and that. Young fellas, they like it too — they work there. We'd go playing, us girls, that's all; little cubby houses — *kankus*. An old lady at Tarcoola, Mrs Roberts, she'd give us the tin to feed the chooks.

Our father was like all Anangu there — going about Anangu ways. He was learning whitefella work and he knew it too. He did some work for old fellas there — woodchopping, digging a hole for rubbish ... He made money.

When that job run out, he'd go away cutting boomerangs. When the train came, on the East–West line Express, those *watis* — men they'd sell the boomerangs; make money — silvers, ten bob.

We made a lot of money in those days.

Back to Kingoonya

But I was always worrying — keep saying, '*Kulpanytjaku* Mummy! I want to go back to Mummy!' Mummy was there with that other old man — stepfather. I wanted to go back to Mummy and Dad. So after that, go back then. 'Come on, we go back to Kingoonya.'

Kingoonya! Oh, lots of cottages, houses, pub, dance hall, big shop. A lot of times we've been there. That's our **home** — Kingoonya!

1. Kingoonya: Early life

Tarcoola
The original town of Tarcoola, established in 1902 during a gold rush, is about two kilometres north of today's railway township. Gold was discovered in 1893 and at the height of the mining rush about 2000 people lived in Tarcoola. An influx of water later stopped further exploration. When Daisy Bates settled at Ooldea in 1919, the Ration Depot was at Tarcoola police station. Soon after she took up camp, Mrs Bates reported a large traditional Aboriginal gathering at Tarcoola — the Kokatha people inhabiting a vast surrounding area. In *The Passing of the Aborigines* (1938) she had strong words about the harm the building of the Transcontinental line had on the traditional owners of the area. 'Each group through whose territory the line was passing saw its waters used up, the tree and bushes destroyed for firewood and fence posts, and the whole country turned to strange uses.' Today at the railway junction of Tarcoola, several houses, a police station, hostel and the Wilgena Hotel remain, patronised by those engaged in renewed mineral exploration. *Photograph: Aboriginal Heritage, DOSAA*

CHAPTER 2
The Travelling: Learning from the Old People

Travelling to Lake Pirinya (Lake Phillipson)

We didn't know about those Old People Walking yet, we didn't know. Mum tell us when we go back there, Kingoonya.

My father, my **own** father come again Kingoonya and he took us with the Old People travelling to Lake Pirinya — whitefellas' name Lake Phillipson.

Mum says, 'He wants to take you girls. You going?'

And stepfather said, 'Yes. Take those girls for a month or two.'

So we came here then to Lake Pirinya travelling on camels. The Old People, those old *tjilpis*, they used to camp there. I seen that right throughout when I was small. We used to have a swim in there, Lake Pirinya.

Those Old Men check it out; 'Don't you kids go there, go over our side.' (Not allowed to go that way.) 'You kids got to go that way!'

Yes those Old People used to camp there. *Kanku* — bush shelter, *kankus* they made there — they put brush on the tree to make it shady. Yes, shady sitting down.

2. The Travelling: Learning from the Old People

Lake Phillipson
Lake Phillipson, 100 kilometres south-east of Coober Pedy, has always been, and continues to be, of traditional sacred importance for Aboriginal people. Part of the lake's importance in the past was as a vital source of fresh water and food when it occasionally filled from the flow of Long's Creek. A soak, still present today, was a constant source of water within the lake area. In modern times, Coober Pedians use it for sailing and other recreational pursuits when it is filled with water. When full, it is a shallow lake which holds water for several years; however, it is usually a dry lake-bed. *Photograph: Garry O'Reilly; CPHS*

Lake Pirinya — Traditional life goes on

Lake Pirinya — full of water. Yes, *ma̱lu* — kangaroos there every day and all hanging up on the tree. Some of them young fellas too go hunting. I don't know what they do to kill the *ma̱lu*. That's the men's job — shoot 'em, I think. After they killed them, they cooked 'em, they cut 'em up and hang 'em out.

They eat that part there.

Emu — they sometimes come — *ka̱laya*.

Old People say, 'Don't you fellas make too much noise!'

They wait for emu too. A lot of sweet tucker they want. *Ka̱laya* to the water and BANG! — kill two or three so a big mob of people can eat.

We fella kids, we just playing in the water, picking eggs there — ducks and swans and all kinds of birds. We can chuck it away that egg or keep it and boil it. Like that. We're not allowed to eat the swans, not allowed. Ducks, that's the one we had — those ducks. Big girls, they get those ducks' eggs — cook 'em.

Everyone, all the A̱nangu, have a feed about late afternoon. They get ready then *inmaku* — for the singsong, for the dance. *Uwa!* Yes! We go — see the pretty things what they're wearing, you know, what they put on for the *inma*.

We thinking, 'What sort of pretty flowers they be putting on?' and the Old Men tell the little ones, the pretty baby ones when they start crying for something, '*Inma nga̱ranyi! Inma* there!'

And some people here now living in Coober Pedy don't know here now that was going on. The people that come late, behind, the latecomers they don't know what's been happening like that with us. **We're** the ones who have been travelling around here!

2. The Travelling: Learning from the Old People

Gathering bush tucker

The collection of *mai*, non-meat food, remains the domain of the women. *Maku*, the witchetty grub, is still highly prized. *Tjala*, the sweet honey ant, is a sought-after delicacy but only obtainable further north of Coober Pedy. Both foods involve much hard digging by women and children. The eggs of swans and ducks and other birds were staple items in earlier times; the photograph shows a swans' nest at Lake Phillipson.

With land clearance and the introduction of European foods, other *mai* has not survived so strongly — for example the *wakati's* (bush seed's) time-consuming yandying process gave way to the use of whitefellas' flour. This new flour, however, was substituted and cooked as damper in the ashes. Quondongs remain a popular bush fruit with bush raisins, wild tomatoes, and wild banana and others less widely prized. *Photograph: Michele Madigan with the guidance of Eileen Crombie*

I'm the one that know this country!

Travelling with camels

Old Wongey

One old fella been give me a camel. My old camel, old Wongey. Me bossy with that camel. Won't give anyone a ride, any girls — 'You ask me if you want a ride.'

Those girls crying, my girlfriends you know, Betty Smith and Lena. When I jump on, they jump on.

My old camel, old Wongey. Old white one; big, white all over, you know. Not like other camels — this one white, old Wongey.

Into Coober Pedy for the stores

We come back here to Coober Pedy, on the camels, every time when they run out at Lake Phillipson, every time when they run out for tea, sugar, flour — enough bags of flour to last.

And one time, going home again, just this side of Eight Mile — *watingku*, men, in front, leading the camels, (this group was full too) and one camel was the young one — Wongey's kid, Tjumbra. And we girls only be small ones, you know. I can't think how old I must be, about ten, maybe.

One of the Old People, Eileen Wingfield's father (poor old *tjilpi* — he looks after us, but he was playing with us this time), — he trained that Tjumbra, 'You chuck these girls off directly', he was whispering in his ear.

And the camel must have heard it, you know. Yeah and he done it! Dogs were playing there on the foot side. You know the camel just pull away and the rope just come off!

There were four of us girls; my sisters Linda and Molly, Irene Dingaman's old mother and me. One in the front and three in the back. Like that. Saddle-sitting, you know — sitting in the saddle. The oldest one was sitting in the back and me in front of her and 'nother one in front of me and 'nother girl my sister, she was sitting in the front there on her own.

2. The Travelling: Learning from the Old People

Station work with camels
As the outback country became taken over by pastoralists, Aboriginal people's main way of remaining on country was to work for the stations, which many of them did.

Before motor vehicles arrived in the outback, camels were used extensively for station transport. Here they are seen being loaded with bales of wool to be sent to market from Purple Downs Station. Charlie Bryant, second from right, worked at Purple Downs in those early 'camel days', before he and his wife Tottie moved to Coober Pedy where he took up opal mining. *Photograph: Ashleigh Wilson*

Falling off on the way home

Packed up with a blanket, we were going to Lake Phillipson and just about sleeping, you know, everybody was. My sister, she was asleep too in the front and a big overcoat was over her.

And that's when the camel pulled away then — pulled away, coming back the wrong way, that camel pulled to go back to Coober Pedy! And, my older sister, she pulled us right off! Yes, she put her *mara*, hand, on the rope and the rope came off, you know — tore away and just broke! And she pulled us off while she fell through.

All of us fall, blanket and all! Never hurt us then.

That camel bolted that way and we standing down on the ground already. Yes, we got frightened too — it frightened us. And my sister, she was over there crying along then; she woke up crying! She fell on the ground. Her old mother cried, running along, there. Then everything was all right. We went on. But we got sulky to sister — that oldest sister, Winnie sitting on another camel, old Wongey. She was laughing so we got sulky and go along.

'What! You going to walk?' she been telling us.

'Yeah!' we said.

The old ladies say, '*Yananyi tjina kulpanyi* — we've got to walk home all together.' And one old lady took us behind all the way home.

We got to Long's Creek, the one waterhole because they watered the camels there. They'd camped there. We coming in as it was a bit dark — walking. (We just walk anyway, you know.)

The Old People is home and everything was all there ready for us — tea; *mai* — bread; and *kuka* — meat: *malu* — kangaroo — and bullock. And *warunya kampanyi* — they're burning the fire all night to welcome us.

Then always be, the Old People always be on the **MOVE!** — they go walkabout. They say, '*Tjitji tjuta!* Little kids! 'We *yananyi* now. We're going along now.'

We go back there — go back to Kingoonya.

2. The Travelling: Learning from the Old People

Nilpinna Tim
Nilpinna Tim, Eileen Wingfield's father, who was also known as Tim Allen, is pictured here with his camel Kathleen, which had a crooked hump. In the early decades of Coober Pedy camels were relied upon for transport. Dogs were also useful as hunters and companions. Some of Coober Pedy's older remaining dugouts are in the hills in the background, near the old government water tank. *Photograph: PIRSA; Anne Johnson*

CHAPTER 3
Coober Pedy: 'I grow up here'

Stepfather on the Netting

Then my old father, my stepfather, he got a job on the Netting fence. One old man Chapman give him a job and help him work and build up to put the Netting here in the line between Ingomar and here; on the Netting and we been with them again — kids.

Chapman's Camp and he walked there, old stepfather with us kids coming along. And we kids mucking about with birds and things, try to catch them and they fly away — they run away. And no netting to catch 'em.

Then he bring all of us in here, Coober Pedy, for tucker. Kids, you know and we don't know nothing about they look for opals or anything like that. We just playing along and go back and have *mai* again — have a feed — and go to bed. They brought us here to Coober Pedy, that's all.

Then **everyone** up here Coober Pedy again. For opal.

3. Coober Pedy: 'I grow up here'

The Dog Fence
The Dog Fence (or Dingo Fence), pictured here at Mabel Creek Station c.1960, stretches for 2225 kilometres across South Australia, while its total length, through New South Wales to Queensland, is 5309 kilometres. Aboriginal people in South Australia usually refer to it as the 'Netting'. As far back as the 1880s, many South Australian pastoral lease holders erected their own dog fences. Dingo scalps were worth 7s 6d [75 cents] but in the 1930s Dr Charles Duguid reported that in the north-west of South Australia many of the 'doggers' gave Aboriginal people 'a handful of flour apiece' for a dingo scalp, for which the doggers then received the full government bounty. Some people saved their scalps for the regular visits of a fair trader such as Jessie Lennon's future father-in-law, Jim Lennon. The *Dog Fence Act 1946* legislated for a connected fence made up of pre-existing fences, to be administered by a Board. The fence was erected to protect th sheep, only cattle were allowed outside the fence. *Photograph: Joe Kennedy; CPHS*

Joining family members in Coober Pedy ... and moving away again

And my sister's daughter, Eileen is down here in Coober Pedy today. Eileen Wingfield, she is now — my oldest sister Winnie's daughter. She was my eldest sister's oldest baby. My eldest sister married the man from Dieri — from that side — east. Married there see and she had them two girls. She lived here, Coober Pedy, before I came. She had a baby and we didn't know — we was there, Kingoonya.

After Kingoonya, then come back to North Well. We know the bosses, Old Mr McBride, he's the owner. Mr Jack Pick, the manager, North Well/Wilgena and my mother and father stopped there more.

That's where we've been — walkabout, sort of, walking around. When we want to come here, we come. They bring us here. Then we go back again — yes to Kingoonya. And my brother, Willie Austin born in Kingoonya there. Railways was there.

Go to another place there again, Coondambo. It's a different one from the one that's there now; Glendambo — it's **this** side of the old one. Old well, old windmills on it. Bore. Coondambo, that's the boundary riders' hut. Whitefellas, *walypalas* — when their husband go to work, they stay there.

And A<u>n</u>angu there before that bitumen road there, getting rations too, that first lot of people before us at Coondambo.

The road

That bitumen road shifted away from Kingoonya. They've made that right. Used to be a little bit bendy one, going to Tarcoola way and turning and coming back this way. The new road comes straight here to Coober Pedy. That's our road, our country, that one. We come here *tjina* — by foot, coming along.

3. Coober Pedy: 'I grow up here'

The Stuart Highway
Before 1980 the Stuart Highway between Port Augusta and the Northern Territory border (the only north–south arterial roadway through central Australia) was nearly all graded dirt road. As the photograph shows, heavy rainfall could close the highway. Apart from emergency medical services by air, station people relied on the highway for transporting and receiving all their goods and services. It was one of the few links to the outside world for Coober Pedy and for twenty-five sheep and cattle stations in this area. The sealed highway completed in 1987 took a more direct route. Although it by-passed Kingoonya and all the homesteads in the area, isolation of the people in the far north of South Australia was greatly diminished. *Photograph: Joe Kennedy; CPHS*

To Kupa Piti for the opal

Anangu, Old People bring us up here. They know when it's closer. They might come halfway from Tarcoola somewhere and sit down and might say, 'Oh, Coober Pedy close too. We've got to *yananyi ngura yankunytja* — got to go to that place!'

They learn then — opal over there. Get the opal. Kupa Piti/Coober Pedy. They sell 'em too. They get 'em and go along, sell 'em just for fruit and apples, like that. I think we had cool drink then too, I'm not sure.

Kids on the dumps

Opal — just get enough to sell 'em. Good opal there too for sell 'em clean and proper way. We sit down and noodle, all down at the dump. Kids, you know — dump work. Money *pulka* — lots of money. We were kids too and girls, going out noodling and bringing it back. We used to climb around on them hills, how they dug out there.

We come around and climb down — go somewhere else. When they throw all the chips down, you know, yes, we sit down and noodle.

3. Coober Pedy: 'I grow up here'

The Big Flat opal field workings
The Big Flat opal field was one of the first areas mined after the initial discovery of opal in 1915, and it was established as the principal field by 1916. The photograph shows miners at work and their hand windlasses. From 1915 until the 1950s it was all hand-worked mining, thus there were only small 'dumps' of dirt. With the introduction of bulldozers in the 1950s, most of these old workings were obliterated. This field's close proximity to the town made it easily accessible, so it would have been a popular place to 'noodle' (go through the dumps of dirt, picking out any bits of opal overlooked by the miners). The Big Flat field is now incorporated into the town area.
Photograph: PIRSA; Anne Johnson

Anangus camping everywhere there in Coober Pedy

There was big open ground along there, all the way around. And right up the ground. Right up to the flat hills, you know. Camping everywhere there. All the A<u>n</u>angu. This in Coober Pedy too, you know — drop their swag anyway.

They always go 'round from the government tank and camp. Some people get a water — camel; walk around there, leading the camel. Not **everybody** — but people like that to come here — they been starting to come here to Coober Pedy to meet people they already know. They been pointing out opals.

We were kids too and girls, going out noodling and bringing it back, straight to that shop down there — one store for everything.

Waiting for the stores

Everything come on mail truck. They hard up to wait for the mail because the mail bringing that flour — flour, tea and sugar. Yes, tea!

Everyone come in. They get the opals. All waiting for mail truck — new building of Desert Cave there now. Waiting, they cook anything there. They cook rabbits there, goannas, anything — waiting. Then happy they were, those cookies.

Old Vic Williamson, old storekeeper. Tucker then, the stores come in; cool drink, apple and oranges. Biscuit — no icecream. And the lollies. Lollies wasn't a good flash lolly what you know they give now. It was a black one — that licorice. And that 'nother — black one again with the mark on it — black and white one — peppermint, you know. Only those lollies we had.

We take a bag full and that's only the one lolly.

3. Coober Pedy: 'I grow up here'

Ooldea people visiting Coober Pedy, 1947
The Aboriginal people pictured here with their cart are from Ooldea, south-west of Coober Pedy, on the East–West rail line. Their cart would have been pulled by either camel or horse, which was a common sight then. Bill Dawson, a visitor from Robe in south-eastern South Australia, is holding one of their spears. Where this photograph was taken is now the centre of the town, and the empty hills in the background are full of both business and residential dugouts. *Photograph: Jen and Mike Lloyd; CPHS*

I'm the one that know this country!

Kind people — old miners living in the dugouts

They didn't have school — no school in Coober Pedy. Just walking in the middle here, all over here. No house. Houses now. Go down this way — Church there now. The dugout was there.

We go down that road. Old man stops there. Old man, whitefella. He's a German. He stopped there and we go in and ask him. We might be playing around — ask him for a drink of water. Good fella and we ask him in a good way too.

'Can we have a water?' Like that. That was a good man stayed there. 'Cause Catholic Church there now. Good man he was. He feed those childrens!

Then lot of people down from Lucas's shop there now — other side. Old *tjilpis* — old people in the dugouts, cooked a lot of tucker for us. We hungry, we can't get nothing. Our Old People not quick enough to cook it. All the *tjitji* — all the kids — got plenty of damper, you know. Yes, he's a good man too, he was. He stop in that dugout not far from Lucas' store there now. One dugout in that hill — that's all the dugouts there was there.

Another lot of dugouts was in the caves down there — Umoona Cave there now. That wasn't a dugout right through at the time but half way.

Bon Bon Station

I was about twelve and we went to Bon Bon Station with the Netting work. Twins Station again.

Someone in the family got sick and gone home to Kingoonya but we stayed at Bon Bon for a long time — with that horse and how to ride 'em and mustering sheeps.

Archie Badenoch, he's our playmate at Bon Bon. We was growing up together. We're the *tjilpis* — Old People — now here in Coober Pedy. Used to give him a hiding; can't give him a hiding now! Make a little cubby house — make out we're cooking potatoes, onions, that's all. We don't know carrots or turnips — we don't know that *mai* — food.

Afterwards we knew it. Then they was in a tin — wartime.

An early miner's dugout
This photograph shows a typical miner's dugout in the 1930s in Bolshevik Gully (in the main street). Dugouts then had crudely dug entrances cut into the hillside and one or two small rooms, with the main furnishings carved from the bed-rock as part of the room. As these were built by hand labour using explosives, pick and shovel, they were necessarily small. Miners came and went casually with the boom and bust times, as well as seasonally, so dugouts were usually abandoned or taken up by newcomers if unoccupied. *Photograph: Mrs Marshall; CPHS*

Back to Coober Pedy

All the time we childrens were coming here. I grow up here, Coober Pedy — grow right up with Eileen Allen (Wingfield). Mother brought us here — Mum coming here. Stepfather wanted to work here too for opal. We stopped here too. I was stopping with my sister Winnie, Eileen's mother after that. My old father come here and go again.

The Old People used to stay here too in Coober Pedy; that part there, right on top there, other side of the tank — north side. Camels there. People coming there. Had the *inma* — traditional dances — there too.

Lake Phillipson was the main place — *kapi* — water there. No Mabel Creek station. No Mount Clarence station. Might have been starting the stations then. Mount Penhryn was a new station.

How Coober Pedy got its name

Old Tottie, Aunty Tottie we called her, Tottie Turner, old woman, Norveen Turner's granny, she came from that way — south. Old Tottie and old George Turner were brother and sister. They were living around here at the time. Later on, when I had Bernard, they told me this story about how Coober Pedy got its name.

Old Tottie and George — they talk 'Kupa' and we-fellas call it *walypala* — whitefella. *Piti* is A<u>n</u>angu *wangka* again — our Aboriginal language — (Ma<u>t</u>utjara). A long time ago, they called this *ngura* — this place — *Kupa Pi<u>t</u>i*: white man's hole in the ground.

That's a good name. They talked about it when they saw the whitefella turning up, you know, looking around. Those swaggies too. Some whitefella must have asked some womens or mans, 'What now? What do you call these diggings?'

Must have asked we-fellas here — old Tottie mob, George Turner. 'Oh, we say, '*Pi<u>t</u>i kupaku*' white mans' hole.'

They must have been writing something down too, I reckon, and it came out, 'Coober Pedy.'

Yes, old George Turner — he named it Coober Pedy.

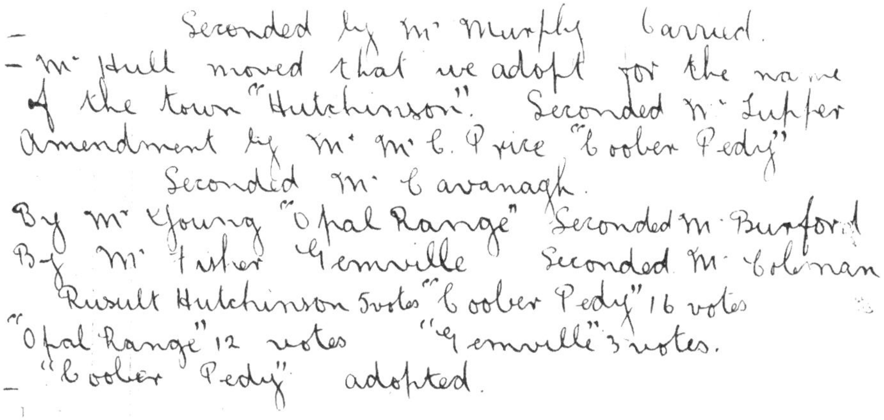

— Seconded by Mr Murphy Carried.
— Mr Hull moved that we adopt for the name of the town "Hutchinson". Seconded Mr Lupfer
Amendment by Mr Mr C. Price "Coober Pedy"
Seconded Mr Cavanagh.
By Mr Young "Opal Range" Seconded Mr Burford
By Mr Fisher "Gemville" Seconded Mr Coleman
Result Hutchinson 5 votes "Coober Pedy" 16 votes
"Opal Range" 12 votes "Gemville" 3 votes.
— "Coober Pedy" adopted.

The Progress Committee

As there were no governing bodies or police, diggers on the field originally known as Stuart Range Opal Field formed a Progress Committee in 1919 to establish some necessary basic rules. The extract of the Progress Committee minutes of June 1920 shown here document how the new name for the town, Coober Pedy, was selected by a vote of sixteen miners. The town continued to be served by a Progress Committee until 1987 when it became a District Council. *Extract: District Council of Coober Pedy*

I'm the one that know this country!

Tottie Bryant

We used to stay at Craters — German Gully. Mum and Dad used to say, 'We go up to Craters' camp. *Kulpanyi* — we'll go back home.'

At night we stay there — cook some *mai* — food.

Mummy and Daddy used to make a camp and old Tottie Bryant (used to be Tottie Turner) used to say to us, 'Nice place up there — I'll come up there, me and my Charlie.'

Tottie and Charlie come up there — get 'em kangaroo and rabbit — always catching rabbits. Had kangaroo dogs, five of them, I think. Good kangaroo dogs. They stay home, look after the mine, wait at the camp, don't run away. Some other silly dogs do run away, eh? But kangaroo dogs can well look after the camp.

Tottie and Charlie, they ready to go shooting. They go out — the dogs on the back all standing along, looking, smelling away! They had a car — a T-model Ford and flat top. The dogs be standing there, side on each side; the dogs be happy as anything, riding along to chase the kangaroo.

Tottie had four lambs there — four lambs or five. They follow the old Tottie. Up they go coming down the street to get some mails and some food. And the lambs behind and some of the dogs follow them too, Charlie and Tottie to old Vic Williamson's store.

They got that big opal down here again too — they got it at Eight Mile. They got it on the Mt Clarence Station road. She seen the opal there, dugged that out.

Later on again, they took her away because she was old. He was old too. They had something wrong with their hands.

Tottie Bryant

In 1946 Aboriginal woman Tottie Bryant was shepherding her few sheep with her dog when she kicked over a stone and revealed an opal. This discovery at what became the Eight Mile field started a rush which opened up an extremely lucrative opal field. Tottie and her husband Charlie Bryant are pictured here in front of their tiny dugout near the old government water tank in Coober Pedy. According to Coralie and Leslie Rees's book, *Australia: The Big Sky Country* (1971), Charlie and Tottie were still hunting kangaroo in their old car in the 1960s, taking along their kangaroo dog and pet lamb, both of which insisted on sharing the front seat with them. *Photograph: John and Shirley Wake; CPHS*

Finding a boyfriend in Coober Pedy

Yes, I grow up here in Coober Pedy, grow right up. I find a boyfriend here — Joe's father. We stayed here and we wasn't worrying about the opal — sitting down.

We'd seen him when he was young, Joe's father. And the old man Jim Lennon — really strict. They had a dugout just down there, where all the dugouts — the new places, flash ones are there now, just down the hill again, Government Tank Hill, they call it. And the little round hill beside it — one dugout there was our home; old father-in-law, his dugout; Irish father-in-law's home. We lived in that — we camped outside — *ngarinyi*. We go in there to have our *mai* — dinner.

They knocked that down now. That's where they been living. They were staying here all the time.

Up comes the Tarcoola policeman

Then they won't allow us to live together because I was young and he was young — like that. We runned away and stayed here and we weren't worrying about the opal. Sitting down.

Up comes the policeman. Tarcoola policeman — he's all right. He just tell him, our stepfather I didn't want to go home. We all used to one another then.

The police lock-up
Residential police were first sent to Coober Pedy in 1921 during an opal dispute. This photograph shows the lock-up and police camp. The first two policemen were transferred away after only one year because needs did not justify their presence. From 1922 until 1965 police had to be called in from Port Augusta, Oodnadatta or Tarcoola. Residential police were re-established in 1965 and in 2000 numbered 15 constables. The corrugated iron lock-up, abandoned by the police, was Coober Pedy's first above-ground building, and it remains today under the protection of the District Council. *Photograph: Department of Mines; CPHS*

Finding out news from the war

No houses right around then. No, nothing. Only a few people — whitefellas sitting down living. Yes, little bits of dugouts everywhere in that hill — north-west hill.

One fellow always sitting down over there, across the creek — dugout. Jenny Gough's dugout there now. Carl Willie, *tjilpi,* sitting down there, night time, with a torch, you know, flicking the light, talking to another fellow — dugout — down there. I watched that.

I asked Joe's father, 'Why those lights be always shining?'

And **he** asks his father, my old father-in-law Lennon, 'Hey — that dugout up there — what's that man talking all the time?' Father-in-law, he laughs then and he been say, 'They **talk** to one another.'

Palumpa tjukurpa kulini — he listens to the news. He's got a wireless there, old wireless I suppose and he come out and he talk on the torch then — *wangka*. They talking about the war been going on, about what's been going on overseas. Father-in-law been in the war before — the Boer War. In Africa. That's how he knows — Joe's Irish grandfather Lennon. Lot of Lennons too. Five brothers — five or six or seven, I think. They had a cattle station up there; one place called Wantjapala, just up from Marla.

We stayed together there then like that for a while, living in the dugout at Government Tank Hill. But after that, Joe's father took me off to the station, Bon Bon Station. On the old mail truck he took me, Mother there to meet me. Mum was growling at me, telling me off, 'You want to get a man when you get older.'

I stopped there then, working. I forgot about Joe's father then.

3. Coober Pedy: 'I grow up here'

Carl Willie
Carl Willie, a miner, is pictured at the entrance to his dugout. Willie arrived in Coober Pedy in the 1920s and lived there for some 30 years. He looked after the Douglas hand pump at the old water tank. According to Tom Ryan, a farmer who came to Coober Pedy to try his luck in the severe drought of 1930, Willie was known as a casanova (Johnson 2006). Not only did he advertise for housekeepers regularly in the Adelaide newspapers, he endeared himself to the small visiting tribes with his really good cooking. People remember that he once tied some special food to a rope, hanging it down a shaft for safe keeping, but when he checked it later he found the food gone and a large rock tied in its place. *Photograph: John and Shirley Wake; CPHS*

I'm the one that know this country!

Working as a single woman

They wanted a girl at Kingoonya — pub — hotel, and we went back to Kingoonya again on the camels. Old People had their camels and one camel for us to ride in.

I been through that — working in the pub, right through. I just wash up, mop the floor, wash the clothes, put it out in the boiler, hang them out …

Didn't travel back this side again. Stayed Kingoonya, *wati wiya* — no man, 'til I find a man.

I came back to the station — some time at Twinsfield (Twins) — at the station I worked. That's the last I worked there. I was a single woman. I had my youngest brother, Jimmy Austin and Tinyma — Billy Pepper, Mindy's father, Pepper; those children to mind. My sister was there — Molly Brown and Tommy Brown with Jack Brown and we been sit down there. Those boys came from Kingoonya.

We went back to Bon Bon — Bon Bon Station after that.

Whitefella women's work

In the station country, girls such as Jessie Lennon had no opportunity for schooling; many took on 'whitefella work' — domestic women's work on stations or in hotels. Jessie, following her mother's example, worked in the Kingoonya Hotel (pictured). Primary schooling was available generally where missions were established, but usually only up to grades three or four for Aboriginal girls. At about the age of 12 or 13 they were expected to work as domestics in cities or country towns.

Mrs Garnett, wife of the Superintendent of Point Pearce Mission, said in her evidence to the Royal Commission on the Aborigines, 1913: The great need in dealing with the girls of the mission is that they be placed out to domestic services as they reach a suitable age ... Personally I feel strongly that ... compulsory systematic placing of them out is necessary ... It would be an expensive thing to train them for cooking and dressmaking. I think that would be putting the Government to needless expense, because there is such a demand for them as raw material. They can all wash dishes and scrub floors. (Mattingley and Hampton 1988) *Photograph: Tony Redden*

I'm the one that know this country!

Joe's father went and found me again

He went and found me again — met up again, coming up the road there, coming back to Twinsfield and we seen him, Joe's father, Barney Lennon, coming in from the north. He come up again on the horse — horse was from Mount Penryhn.

Yes, and we pulled up. Old Jack sing out — Jacob Santing — 'There's your boyfriend coming!'

'Get up and drive on!' I tell him off.

I was down, blanket down, laying. The two boys were talking, my brother, Jimmy and my brother–cousin, Mindy's father, Pepper.

Barney Lennon pulled up and talked and he turned around talking to me. Then whispering away, 'What about we meet one another. Go away. Not running around here all the time. Go away and get married. *Ini?*'

And, '*Uwa*,' I said. '*Uwa!* — Yes!'

I come back, work for a little while and got my pay. He packed up and left where he was — Miller's Creek Station near Coward Springs. He came up on the Boss's car to Kingoonya — to his father's place; old Jimmy Lennon's place. I didn't pack up. I just left it, the job, then. We jumped on the same truck.

3. Coober Pedy: 'I grow up here'

Jacob Santing's mail run
Although he was somewhat disabled, and drove only a dilapidated old truck, for twenty-five years Jacob Santing delivered the mail, freight and passengers (who squeezed in or piled on top) from the railway at Kingoonya to Coober Pedy, and served all the stations in between as well. During the 1930s, Santing's weekly round-trip of 800 kilometres provided Coober Pedy with its only link to the outside world. During his absence through the week, Minnie Berrington and Vic Williamson, both opal miners, ran the store. All three were highly regarded by the eighty miners in Coober Pedy (half of whom were over 50-years-old), and many survived on credit at the store. The store and the old police lockup were the only above ground buildings at that time. Santing is pictured here in 1948. Two of his passengers are Linda Brown and Ida Lang. *Photograph: Len Beadell; Aboriginal Heritage, DOSAA*

CHAPTER 4

Epic journey: 'That's our honeymoon trip'

Getting married in Port Augusta

Yes, we left that Billy Pepper behind and went to Port Augusta. Policeman come there to Gladstone Square, asking us where we was going. They get really touchy for young girls. Joe's father get frightened thinking, 'Oh, we must go home then.' But the policeman told the Minister to come and find us. In the square there, Gladstone Square, we were sitting there. He came along and he called us back then.

'You married?' he said to me.

We were married Anangu — Aboriginal way. We were meaning business now — running away!

'You better marry her,' he said.

They rang my sister (Rocky's mother) at that Mission — Umeewarra. That was my sister, Linda, my older sister. She from up this side — her mother born at Tallaringa. She married the Dieri man then — from that side, east side — George Mungeranie. Rocky's mother and grandmother lived there at Umeewarra. Yes, my sister and my brother-in-law coming there to see me get married — witnesses. Yeah, we got married; they married us there. Not at the Brethren — just anyway Church. And that was all right.

Told us — asked us, where we going then. Told them that we going to Finniss Springs.

'That's good. You can take Jessie now — look after her.'

That's all. That's the finish of it now. We can't come back here — Coober Pedy.

4. Epic journey: 'That's our honeymoon trip'

Port Augusta
Port Augusta, at the northern end of Spencer Gulf, was an important area for Aboriginal people. With the coming of the settlers, the port became an outlet for wool shipment, the first being in the early 1850s. The town was surveyed in 1854 and named after the wife of the then Governor of South Australia. By the time it was proclaimed a city in 1963, Port Augusta had become an important regional railway centre and the site of a large power station. Gladstone Square (pictured), in the middle of the town, has long been a social gathering place.

The demise of the Commonwealth Railways and other industries has seen the town's population decrease. It remains an important regional location for government offices, and the beauty of the nearby Flinders Ranges and its 'Gateway to the Outback' position have ensured a growing tourism industry. *Photograph: Isobel White; AIATSIS*

The honeymoon trip

We went to this one place, Finniss Springs Mission. We never been there before — Arabana Homeland. That's our **honeymoon** trip! Got to Marree first and went straight on the train to Alberrie Creek Siding. All the people working on the line and the road coming straight to Finniss Springs.

Later on, we get worried then. We both sitting down in the sandhills, hiding. And one young fella again — Topsy Jebydah's uncle said, '*Katja!*' (He called my husband, 'Son' A̱nangu way.)

'*Katja!* Come on! *Kulpanytjaku!*' (Talking *Kulpanytjaku* and that country was a long way away!) '*Kulpanytjaku!* Let's go back home!'

'Can't!' we said. 'We can't travel!' (Winter time — water everywhere laying.)

I had no kids then.

But then we were saying, 'Yes, we can go back — we can! *Kulpanyi tjina* — walking. We know the country.

'I can picture it,' my old man said, my husband. I thought — just over there. Might be four or six miles or something. I just don't know.

Morning time, old Roy Allen and Jessie Stewart from old Renee Stewart's mob there; and Jessie, she cooked the damper for us — *mai* — breakfast. I don't know nothing, I was sleeping. And he been telling, 'Cook a damper, *kangku̱ru* — sister–cousin. *Kulpanyi ngura-kutu!* — we're going back home!'

Walking back

We **did** walk back. Dad (husband) didn't know the country, coming back from Finniss Springs, back to Parakylia way. He was a young fella then. Jack Dolmyer, Topsy Jebydah's uncle, **he** knew the country. He could recognise the sandhills — mustering there for sheep and that. (And later on, my *katjas* — sons — used to call over to him, 'Jack Dolmyer! Come over here!' They got used to his name. They liked that name!) His A̱nangu name was Kaayi — I remember that, they called him that. We'd all been kids together.

4. Epic journey: 'That's our honeymoon trip'

The beginning of Finniss Springs Mission
Due to lack of water and because it was overrun by rabbits, the early far north-eastern South Australia missions of Kopperamanna (Moravian) and Killapanina (Lutheran) closed by 1917. The people from these missions moved mainly to nearby stations and ration depots including Finniss Springs Station, 72 kilometres from Marree. In 1937, the very experienced missionary Annie Lock made a recommendation to the board of the United Aborigines Mission (UAM) in Adelaide to establish a mission at Finniss Springs. Station boss, Mr Francis Dunbar Warren, consented and gave practical support to the venture. By the end of 1942, about three years before Jessie Lennon's 'honeymoon trip', 26 square kilometres of country was 'made over to the UAM for mission use'. The photograph shows some of the traditional Aboriginal shelters at Finnis Springs still standing, many years after their original use. *Photograph: H. Basedow; AIATSIS*

I'm the one that know this country!

The trip back — Finniss Springs to Parakylia

Yes, Kaayi knew the country and he knew how to do whitefellas' work too. He knew the station where he been work — that station we going to. He could recognise the sandhills from when he was mustering for sheep and that.

He showed us — 'Hey! Look like I know that sandhill over there and all the trees, like pine trees. (Not like **real** pine trees, they are.) Look like them pine trees like what I been walking around, young 'un then,' he said.

He been say, '*Yankunytjaku yananyi!* Come on then! Get going before we get tired!'

He was frightened of me that I would start to get slow, you know and don't go fast — keep up to him. I walk along. Yeah, stay behind, coming along.

'Come on, we go along. Look like a windmill over there.' He say, like that.

Water was there. And I was walking along. I feel a bit happy again, walking along.

That was that far from the station all right! Far from the Netting.

Kaayi goes on ahead

Later on, Jack, he been go, he went to that Netting. And my old man said, 'I'll sit down here and have a spell here — wait for her to get better.' Looks like he don't like going to the station.

And I was sitting down and he was digging hole.

I wanted to dig all those *tjunkul tjunkuls* — water root plants. 'Yes,' I been tell him a bit cheeky way, 'Dig that 'nother one over there. *Tjawala tjunkul tjunkuls!* Dig those water roots!' And he been digging them, you know.

4. Epic journey: 'That's our honeymoon trip'

Water in the desert
This 1948 photograph, showing men preparing the ground for another new tank, reflects the continual preoccupation of the Finniss Springs Mission with the problem of finding water; the annual rainfall was approximately 500 points. Lack of water lead to the closure of the Finniss Springs Mission in 1961, after nineteen years in operation. Aboriginal people needed all their knowledge of any available soaks, rock holes, crab holes, water root trees, water bearing plants or *tjunkul-tjunkuls* (water roots), to travel a region such as this in their traditional manner, living off the land. The non-Aboriginal community's lack of this knowledge has led to a sometimes common belief (which continues to astound present-day Aboriginal people in outback regions) that there was no previous Aboriginal presence in the area because no water existed. The desert people's traditional way of life ensured their intimate knowledge of the land, reinforced by their knowledge of the *Tjukur* — the Law of the area. *Photograph: R. Pearce, UAM; AIATSIS*

I'm the one that know this country!

The trip back — Parakylia to Roxby Downs

And I could see him worrying too. 'And that fella suppose to run over there to that tree what he knows. And he supposed to come back and tell us straight away. But from there he run into that road there and the Netting gate was there and he went into the **station**. He didn't come back! To let us know!'

So we followed the station road. We followed him where he went. Oh, we had a little bit of a row with him — up and tell him off.

But the Bosses, they were already there — waiting for me and him with that food, blankets and that. We can camp there. *Waru* — fire going there, big fire going there. Kaayi cooking sheep's head and that. And he told us. (Oh, no wonder he gone, kept going — he catch up with somebody's motor car and he go!)

We come right **in!** Yeah, we walked right in from Finniss Springs to Parakylia!

Parakylia Station — we sat down there and in the morning, they give us breakfast. Give him a boot.

Got his boots and 'We're right!' And then that station owner, that old *tjilpi* — old man, Dave Greenfield, he give us a ride on the bus — mail bus come and we're going to another stop then — another station — Roxby Downs. The Boss, he told us about the Bosses at those stations — Parakylia and Roxby Downs, they were two brothers.

At Roxby Station we went on the mail bus to get on the train. We pack up again that night.

4. Epic journey: 'That's our honeymoon trip'

Roxby Downs

In the 1980s, part of the Roxby Downs station became a township (1998 pop. about 4000) and a mine. The controversial *Roxby Downs Indenture Ratification Act 1982* committed the South Australian Government to facilitate the mining at Roxby Downs of refined copper and associated products — uranium, silver and gold. At the end of the 1995–96 financial year, the South Australian Government reported that the infrastructure costs to the government at that date were $10 million more than the royalties received. The original joint venturers were Western Mining and British Petroleum (who withdrew in 1993). The mine will use 42,000,000 litres of water a day from the Great Artesian Basin, as recent legislation has allowed the Olympic Dam expansion project to go ahead, making it the largest uranium mine in the world. The further proposed new expansion for 2010–11 by the current operators BHP Billiton, plans to use 100,000 litres of water per minute from the Great Artesian Basin and the proposed desalination plant on Spencers Gulf.

Len Beadell's photograph taken at Roxby Downs Station in 1961 includes Ettie Eyres (station boss' wife), her children and 'Zainabi Khan's Aunt' (domestic helper). *Photograph: Len Beadell; Aboriginal Heritage DOSAA*

Waiting at Wirraminna

Wirraminna Siding — Wirraminna Station just out from there. Siding there and station there too, but we not going to the station. Siding is where the train arrive in. We sat down there and he said, 'We sit down here all day 'til the sun goes down a bit. We go up to the siding then. We might find a room on the train.' Just out from the siding, we get a big bush; nice warm sunny morning like winter time, you know, you always like a bush there, warm place. So we sat down, had a little bit of a feed.

We were going along then, walking slowly and we can see some fire going in the shed there. All the sleepers there — wood — they've got a shed there. The people that lived there made the shed like that. And this one fellow there — a traveller again; hitchhiker again. He had his fire going and he was cooking and we was going and he must have heard us and he come out.

'Oh, hello, mate! Come here. I got a nice big fire here.'

And we was *ngu̱lu* again — frightened, thinking he must be *ngunytji* — tricking us. He must be a killer. And he said, 'Aye — sit down there. It's cold.' He got a cup of tea and all there. He was waiting for the train going to Kalgoorlie way.

So we sat down.

Jumping the train

Then we see the lights coming — long way. Oh go a long way then. Waiting then. It's the fast goods. Big fast train, that one. It's our train going through there. We've got to catch that **fast** train. '*Uwa!* — Yes,' I was thinking, 'we'll jump on somehow!'

And that train just come **in**.

It came there, the engine part — we seen it come down there. He pull up there and he just come along then. He must have just picked up something there — a parcel or something or drop it off. And we thought he was just going to pull up again. But he picked that up there and he just going through. He was getting faster — not fast, you know — just going.

And he said, 'Hey, he's going! Think you could jump on?'

And he jumped on!

4. Epic journey: 'That's our honeymoon trip'

The rise and demise of the sidings
With the establishment of the Ghan and the East–West (Transcontinental) railway lines, railway sidings, such as Wirraminna (pictured in 1945), became increasingly common across the north of South Australia. In the 1920s, between Tarcoola and Ooldea, there were only two sidings — Wynbring and Barton. This later grew to seven. Sidings such as Wirraminna took the name of the station property through which they ran. Until the 1960s there were still many Transcontinental railway towns, each with about a hundred people. The installation of concrete sleepers began the real demise of the sidings and towns. This continued with the growth in express traffic, mechanisation and job rationalisation, and in 1998 the last remaining township of Cook was abandoned. *Photograph: W. Tippett; Aboriginal Heritage, DOSAA*

Kalpa! Climb up!

Yes he asked me so, calling out, '*Kalpa!* Jump up! Yes, you *kalpa!*' And I been *ngalya-kalpanyi*, climbing up towards him. There, you know, the tarpaulin laying down over the load. And I got the rope, see — I hold the rope there, standing then, my *tjina* — foot, down there where something there can hold it. 'There!' he said. 'Now come along now.' (We in between the trucks now. He standing up sideways in the middle, you know.) I been game. I'd been thinking, 'Yes, I'll try the train out.' Just going along, being strong, you know. And he had an old bag too — that's our rug to cover us up. Standing there and he said, 'You right?'

'Yeah, I'm right. Where you want to put me?'

And he said, 'Jump up there, now!'

And that tarpaulin — it was — it was all straight down. You got no hollows there, nowhere to lay down. Rope laying across again. Yes, two ropes. He seen it I suppose. And he been like take hold of me. He sort of turned me there, you know.

And I nearly went over!

He just grabbed me again. Then grabbed the rope again. So we layed along then, hanging on to one another to Kingoonya, hanging on to one another, *wilurara*, going west.

And all the time on that train, I just hang on, hang on, laying down. I didn't watch or look.

I laying down thinking, 'Good job I didn't hit that ground.' That's what I was thinking all the way. And he wouldn't have seen me there. He wouldn't have found me there.

But he say, 'I would have jumped out too!'

Back home at Kingoonya

Kingoonya, the train pulled up, quick one. Jumped down quick way again. Go all around the engine and go home — *ulparira* — south side. We ran into his father up there, his old Irish father — old Jim Lennon, Joe's grandfather.

'Oh!' he said, 'Oh!' He was that happy too. He grabbed us and loved us up and said, 'I'm glad you've come back. I thought I lost you two!'

The decline of Kingoonya
Kingoonya's population began its decline in the 1970s with the appearance of concrete railway sleepers which required little maintenance. At that time it still had a hotel roadhouse, police station, post office, shop, school, racecourse (pictured here in the late 1960s), and a number of houses, particularly for the fettlers. The final blow came in the 1980s when the Stuart Highway was re-routed away from Kingoonya and straightened while being surfaced with bitumen. The hotel closed in 1982 with the new Glendambo hotel, 40 kilometres west, opening on the new highway the next day. Now really in a ghost town, the hotel where Jessie Lennon worked in the early 1940s, is again being used — as a bed and breakfast for passing travellers. *Photograph: Joe Kennedy; CPHS*

CHAPTER 5

Settling down: Going for opal

Doing whitefella work

We sat there for a while — Kingoonya, and we been get a job back there again — Wirraminna Station. They was looking for men, the station owner was looking for men. Ran up to Kingoonya there and the father, Old Jim Lennon, brought back the word — 'Somebody want somebody there at Wirraminna — station work.'

'*Ai!* I'll go there, Dad!'

We went back then and work. I don't know how long we went there — one year. They put us on the train again; from the siding. Carriages — we get in the carriages this time. And we got off there and the station owner picked us up — already sitting there and waiting.

So we stayed there and had our married life there, sitting down. Good time there, going out for kangaroo and you know they driving out for everything — mustering sheep.

My little company

There was a big shed and in the end room, I sit down there where I had a little company — a *ka̲laya* — an old emu. He'd come back. I'd cook a damper, you know. Put it on the table and I'm going somewhere, doing some work somewhere outside; washing or something, hanging clothes out — out on the line.

Walk back, you know. Nothing!

'Oh, he's there, eating my damper.'

Friend he is.

He follow me when I go for a walk. Long way there again. Young, he was, not really big. He played a lot — chasing the motor bike and that. Him chasing the dog. The dog chasing him.

And then, that *ka̲laya* was eating the hot **coals** from the fire! 'Go away!' I'd tell him. 'The coals will cook you in there and I'll eat **you** then!'

5. Settling down: Going for opal

Doing whitefella work

For decades the sheep and cattle industries of South Australia relied heavily on the labour of the Anangu. In 1939 H. Waverly, UAM missionary at Oodnadatta, wrote what seems to be an excellent summary: The work of the natives consists mainly of 1) shepherding goats; 2) shepherding sheep; 3) general stock work such as track riding, killing, branding, mustering, trucking, going with a plant to bring down a fresh mob of cattle generally about 1,500 head; 4) helping generally on the station to pump water, cement tanks, sink bores (for water), build storeyards, attend all musters and count out all own cattle etc., peg out skins, make hobbles; 5) the women generally help in the homesteads, cooking, washing clothes and dishes; 6) Some, but very few, help in the shearing season on the stations which carry sheep. (Mattingley and Hampton 1988) To this the authors would add that a number of women in the Coober Pedy area and elsewhere, also shepherded the sheep and worked on other outside jobs including stockwork. The 1975 photograph shows ringers from Anna Creek and nearby stations. From left: Richard Nunn, Norman Rosella, Raymond Finn, Sammy Brown and Robert Hele (partially hidden). *Photograph: Peter Caust; DOSAA*

I'm the one that know this country!

Going off to the opal fields

And after that, the station owner put him off then, put him off from working there. We thought about going to Kingoonya again. *Ka<u>l</u>panytjaku* — we'll jump on the train and we'll go back home, Kingoonya. We went back home to Kingoonya and sat down.

Stayed at Kingoonya for a while and saw one *tji<u>l</u>pi*, the father, old Jim Lennon and say, 'You're going, we're all going today to Eight Mile.'

'They going to Coober Pedy? What for?'

'Opal. Opal there at Eight Mile.'

We told him — 'We'll go and find a dugout — a place for you to live.'

We talk about it and we go then, yeah, we go.

We had to **roll** the swag up then too. Put it on this wagon — big wagon, camel wagon one old *tji<u>l</u>pi* had — old Dickie Thomas, you know. And he give us a ride. We sort of travelling — whole A<u>n</u>angu mob travelling, kids and all.

And the wagon been breaked down!

Broke down at the ramp out from Kingoonya.

All the other A<u>n</u>angus just there: Edna Williams' old father and mother and my old *mama* — father — we were walking around eating *kampu<u>r</u>aras* — desert raisins. Joe's father got a ride — went back for the wagon part. We all sat down eating *ma<u>l</u>u* — kangaroo, waiting for the wagon part to come.

Then they came back with the part — an axle or something like that.

5. Settling down: Going for opal

Heading for Coober Pedy
An Aboriginal family travelling the track heading to Coober Pedy in May 1946. Camels were used commonly as transport here well into the 1950s. This form of transport would be very similar to that used by Jessie Lennon and her family. They were not only ridden or pulled wagons such as this one, they also packed water from far away, before there was a more permanent supply from the water tank built in 1921. *Photograph: PIRSA; Anne Johnson*

Getting a fencing job along the way

But someone was sitting down there — this other old fellow; old *tjilpi* again — A<u>n</u>angu — old Aboriginal bloke, Arthur Baker. His camp was just there. A fencer he was. He was just sitting down there, fencing the fence. He was the boss on his own for that fence. And he said, 'Oh, *katja* — nephew — you want a job?' And he gave him the job. He told him properly. He said, 'You take this job. You work with me. I'll give you money. I'll give you the carthorse — horse and cart, that *nyantju* and the cart.'

And we was that **happy!** That Arthur Baker, he was telling me ... he was giving me that horse and cart — '*Palyo!* Oh, that's **good!**'

(I didn't talk like that though. I hid my head, shy way. I was only young at that time. We didn't talk straight out to people's faces like *watiku* — to a man.)

We went back first to the siding — Kingoonya. He had to go back — to change the money, to get fruit and tinny meat. He took them old men back too because we got that job.

At Bon Bon Station

We camped there then — I was happy back there at Bon Bon Station. Arthur Baker's woman was old China Baker. She had an Aboriginal mother. She was kind to me. I was vomiting — sick; can't eat anything.

She said, 'Must be my granny (grandchild Aboriginal way) coming!' And she cooked a feed for me, gave me some milk.

'There you are, girl,' she said.

Then I got all right.

Joe's father done the fencing right around. He got money from that old *tjilpi*. We got tucker, nice tucker too. Yes, he done the fencing right around and he give him the money — pay him. Tell him — 'I'll send you away now. You and your girl can go back there to Coober Pedy now.'

He was hurrying to get away too — come back this way. Lonely again — wanted to come back this way to Coober Pedy. We took off altogether then.

5. Settling down: Going for opal

Working on the stations
H.G. Waverley of the UAM at Oodnadatta in 1939 commented: The problem of work for the natives does not exist here — there is any amount of work for them on the stations — the problem is to get them a fair wage for their work ... Wages — these vary; Some obtain 5s a week — very often less — others 10s and the best 15s a week ... In this state the natives receive just what their employers care to give them ... If they are badly treated they do as I am repeatedly telling them — just leave. (Mattingley and Hampton 1988)

Emily Austin (Barney Lennon's sister), however, in *Stories from Anangu of Coober Pedy* (Skewes 1997), gives a frightening account of her family's attempt to leave Evelyn Downs station when she was a child. As the family escaped from ill treatment, the 'boss' had armed police out looking for them. They were saved by the actions of their cousin, the police tracker. Others, as in Jessie Lennon's account, had a good working relationship.

The photograph shows a cattle yard at Mabel Creek station. *Photograph: Marie Nourse*

On the road again to Coober Pedy

We even went to Twinsfield.

I was carrying Bernard, see. Bernard, a long way coming ... Some reckon, 'You lucky. You don't get sick on the road like that — with the camel or the buggy.'

Oh, some people told me that. Some are like that, you know — get sick.

We come all the way, all the way driving. We come to one bore there out at Twins there, just out of Twins there. We load up water and he asked the station owner, 'Eh, where this Twinsfield Station?' We went to Twinsfield. We pick up plenty of tucker.

We go on for opal then — for the opal field.

I getting tired. 'Hey, when will we get there? Where are we going to? — *Ngura yaaltjiku?*'

'We'll be there, we'll be there,' he said.

He'd go along walking. He'd leave old Molly, the horse, with the cart, on the road. He'd go self on the road, go walking self on the road, go along looking for rabbits. *Uwa!* Yes!

Up there then, Mount Penrhyn we're coming to. We walked close to Brumby Creek road. Come straight into it. Camp half way — camp by the fire. And we're coming to Mount Penrhyn Field — opal field back there.

5. Settling down: Going for opal

Coober Pedy in 1947
The lower main street shown here was only a dusty track through Bolshevik Gully. The store was in the hillside in the background, and there were dugouts nearby. In these early days, Coober Pedy was not a centralised entity; it was scattered over several hectares and had only a few basic facilities: the store, the water tank, and the dugout post office/bank agency. Miners lived where they worked, at the various fields, some of which were located many kilometres distant. *Photograph: Jim Cameron; CPHS*

Meeting relations on the way

Come along, we come along and somebody was travelling along that way: a camel and a man and a woman sitting on the camel. And a little chick — boy — was sitting on the camel going to Twinsfield there. I was sitting on the cart behind our horse, Molly. We come out from around the hill and we saw them.

'We'll meet them.' (That's what I was thinking.) 'We'll get there too. We'll all meet 'em.'

And then I said, 'That's my sister! My sister Molly!' That was their little boy, Jack Brown, sitting on the camel.

Oh they was glad.

'Oh I didn't know that was you! *Ngalya yananyi!* Come here!' *Paluru* — she — been saying to him, Tommy Brown — 'relations again'.

(Tommy Brown was my brother-in-law, poor thing. They've all gone now. I've got the sons all right. They're all my children now. They've got sons at Ayres Rock. Tommy's father had a lot of relations. Nothing and nobody left now.)

'Which way we going? Camping here?'

'Ah — Coober Pedy. We going Coober Pedy. For opal. For cool drink.'

5. Settling down: Going for opal

Hand mining in 1947
Jim Cameron, posing here in his mine, mined for opals at the Eight Mile Field for about seven months in 1947. All mining was done by hand, and if a windlass was not used for hauling out the dirt, it was done by shovel. Jim could throw from four metres deep, but he remembers Bill Ryan from Kalgoorlie could throw the dirt from six metres. Jim lived at Eight Mile in a tent, under which he had dug the dirt out to a metre below ground level. Later, another miner took it out below where Cameron had stopped and made a good opal find.
Photograph: Jim Cameron; CPHS

Back at Coober Pedy

We came back here then to Coober Pedy. Straight over to the shop — got some food at the old time shop where the new building is now, Desert Cave. (Before that it used to be called Koska's Hill.)

It **used** to be called Vic's — old Vic Williamson's. He was the old storekeeper, old German *tjilpi*. He know the kids, knew all of us. *Uwa* — yes, a little while and then he seen me married — have a man.

He come and tease me then.

'Oh, little Jessie been here, little one and now she's a big Jessie now — married.'

Uwa — yes, like that, old Vic Williamson been saying to me. I'd be laughing. '*Tjilpi*, don't! You make me shamed!' He's a good old *tjilpi*, good old man. He like me. He been give me cool drink and fruit. And cake; yeah present, wedding present that cake and that was good! Bullock meat too. He knew us.

We were coming back to **stay** then.

5. Settling down: Going for opal

The store in 1946
Miners are waiting here at the store for the arrival of Jacob Santing's mail and goods truck from Kingoonya on a Saturday afternoon in 1946. At this time the store was run by Alf Turner of Mabel Creek Station, who brought his fresh beef in to sell weekly. The dugout to the left held medical supplies and a radio for contacting the Flying Doctor at Ceduna (down on the coast) or for sending telegrams. Keith Wright, who took this photo, came from Melbourne with his father after hearing of the big opal strike at the Eight Mile Field. He estimates there were then approxmately eighty people on the opal fields. *Photograph: Keith Wright; CPHS*

I'm the one that know this country!

Living in the dugout in Coober Pedy

We liked Coober Pedy.

We just got in the dugout down the hill — Government Tank they called it and the little round hill beside it. (A lot of people stopping there now — they've got dugouts — flash nowadays ones!)

And one dugout was our home — old father-in-law's dugout, Jim Lennon. He'd come up to Coober Pedy. We went back to Kingoonya specially to pick him up. We lived in that dugout — in the round hill (And now they got a dugout right up the top of our old dugout.)

We camping **outside** *ngarinyi* — *kunkun* — sleeping outside. We go in there to have our *mai* — dinner.

And down below, in the brush sheds, I had my washing — laundry you might say, I suppose; in the brush shed and I had my tub, buckets of water and a hose to get the water out, you know, to wash my clothes. Me and my cousin, Irene Dingaman's mother. My sister, Molly Brown come there too.

No buildings, all dugouts you know; they all around. Good dugouts, all dugouts there around the hill. And now they've been pushing the big dumps along now, this way, that way and there's a dugout in the middle of it now where we used to walk — where we walked from here to the shop. It's all a different place now. That old white hill where we lived, now it's all knocked around.

All the blackfellas lived out there — playing about, camping — fire going and cooking tuckers; blackfellas' *ngura* — camp; all the Anangus — Aboriginal people.

5. Settling down: Going for opal

An early dugout
The little white hill (shown here) called Government Tank Hill, near the old water tank, later became known as Piazza Hill when Italian miners came to live in the dugouts in the 1950s and 1960s. The camel driver, George Morousen, lived in the dugout on the right, and Tottie and Charlie Bryant's small dugout was nearby to the left of this photo. which was taken in the mid-1940s. An Adelaide newspaper reported this dugout was the store in Coober Pedy in its earliest years. *Photograph: Department of Mines; CPHS*

I'm the one that know this country!

Going out to Eight Mile

Just around the white hill was a dugout. Another old fella again, that was old George Morousen's house. And he carts some water for all the peoples that stop there — **out** where they're camping out. We went out there too, out to Eight Mile.

We all talked up to George Morousen, all the A<u>n</u>angus — we've got to have water out at Eight Mile.

I was big for Bernard then. Go anyway, riding around. Old father, Jim Lennon, used to go out too. Old husband used to get a turkey too — *kipa<u>r</u>a* — and old father used to cook it up.

We come back when it's a week. Come in to Coober Pedy for *mai* — food and old Barney had to clean up the opal and sell it. And go back again.

All the time I been moving.

Old father was at Eight Mile right up 'til I had my first. Bernard first. Then he came in here then to Coober Pedy to the round hill there — that's our home.

George Morousen
George Morousen, of Afghan descent, is shown with his team of draught horses and the wood and metal-wheeled buckboard, with which he carted goods and water to Coober Pedy until 1959. He was a well-known, respected camel and horse team driver around Coober Pedy for many years, delivering firewood and water to dugouts. *Photograph: Jenny Gough*

I'm the one that know this country!

The birth of Bernard

You know, long time people, they have the baby in **their** way, A<u>n</u>angu way. Yes, it's crying and that's all you know.

And peoples is all around my tent there waiting for Bernard to born you know and I had all my sisters around me. Nursing you know — rubbing me down and sitting in the **back** there — *nga<u>lt</u>utjara* — poor thing. They take it in turns to watch where the baby going to come out — might come out the wrong way.

Yes, they could see me — I was starting to get, you know, tired of it. They get *ngu<u>l</u>u* too — frightened; might lose it. Yes Bernard was born there, Eight Mile. I was sick. Doctors *wiya* — no doctors. And the girls or the sisters — **my** sisters was here. My sister-in-laws, sisters of my old husband were there, Tillie Waye, Emily Austin, Millie Taylor too. Millie Taylor, she was working, making the feed for us, working at Mabel Creek.

It was dangerous so my old father — he was a *ngaka<u>r</u>i* — traditional healer — he came in and straightened the foot in the *tjuni* — in my tummy — the foot, the *tjina* was the wrong way. He turned the baby around, right round. And Bernard was born *ku<u>r</u>u pati* — with his eyes shut.

The Willis Family

The Willis family were well-known identities in the Coober Pedy/Kingoonya area. Tommy Willis was born in 1908 in the Pampas Hotel in Port Augusta of Irish parents. He worked as a station hand at Kokatha, near Kingoonya in the 1940s, while Gracie Johns was working in the Kingoonya Hotel, the centre of social gathering for the region, particularly on race weekend when 'everyone would meet up and socialise' at the races and at the dance. Tommy and Gracie married in Port Augusta and the wedding was written up as front page headline news in the Port Augusta press as 'the first white man to marry a "full blood" Aboriginal woman'. The marriage also ensured that their eleven children were protected from being taken away. The couple went up to Eight Mile working together on mining opal, then moved to Bon Bon Station where Tommy worked as a fencer and the family lived for thirty years with their canopied truck as their bedroom. Photographed in 1947 in Coober Pedy are (l to r) Johnny Johns, Joycie Johns with baby Josie, Dorothy Lennon (Jessie's sister-in-law), Gracie Willis (nee Johns) holding Kevin, Billy Lennon (Dorothy's brother) and Tommy Willis Sr. Tommy Willis Jr is the oldest of the ten surviving children.
Photograph: Jen and Mike Lloyd; CPHS

I'm the one that know this country!

Ma Wilson

Old Mrs Wilson too; Ma Wilson — she did the nursing again. As soon as Bernard was born, they got her too. She come up and down to me, you know, to see how we got on. She was busy working, you know; going down there from Eight Mile into the shop down here in Coober Pedy and going to ringing up here and talking to the doctor all the time about me.

And the doctor couldn't get away quick enough to come, to come up here to get me straight away for Bernard when I had labour pains. No phone. There was, what do you call 'em? — a two-way radio. And she go there — post office — talking.

And Ma Wilson used to get the mail for Eight Mile. Poor old Wilson was there at Eight Mile getting the opal. He goes out digging the opal and can't find it.

Emily's birth

Later on again, Emily was born in Kingoonya.

Only the white women came and seen me then. Only one night that time to have Emily. The Lord was giving me Emily — no trouble.

5. Settling down: Going for opal

The Wilsons
Bert and Ethel 'Ma' Wilson came from the Eight Mile Field into Coober Pedy in 1947, not long after the birth of Bernard Lennon. They had bought the store from Young and Russell who had it for only a short time. It was on this site, where the Desert Cave Hotel now stands, that Bert Wilson built the above-ground house (pictured). Ma Wilson had ten children, of whom George (pictured) was the youngest. She drove the big truck to keep their store supplied, and also found the time to nurse the sick and injured and run the pedal wireless for contacting the Royal Flying Doctor. *Photograph: Len Beadell; Aboriginal Heritage, DOSAA*

I'm the one that know this country!

Stanley is born

We growed up the children, me and him.

We were at Eleven Mile when Stanley was born with his hairlip and all that. Four days after, we took him to Mrs Bert Wilson. She been looking after him. We had nothing to give him to drink — he can't suck my *titi* — breast. She must have had a little milk bottle. She had him for three days and doctor told us to take him, doctor from Alice Springs; take him to hospital. They couldn't take him up in the air — he'll die.

We only had a horse and cart and we needed to take him quicker. So this man got us a truck and said, 'Take your baby to the hospital'.

At night he had a sleep — we rolled him up and went to Port Augusta. Stanley didn't cry. Only in the morning he cry.

I left him there in Port Augusta. He's an Umeewarra boy (refer to p.103 for further detail). (Later my daughter's been talking — 'We should have sent for him.')

We rushed straight back and lived at Twelve Mile then. After that we took the old man again, old Jim Lennon; we took him and put him on the train.

We stayed there at Twelve Mile but that's where the bomb caught us …

5. Settling down: Going for opal

Turner's meat delivery at Eight Mile
Alf Turner is shown here at the Eight Mile Field in 1947 off-loading fresh meat from his station, Mabel Creek, which was 40 kilometres away to the north-west. Every Friday he stopped at the Eight Mile on the way to his store in Coober Pedy where he sold fresh meat to the miners. *Photograph: Jim Cameron; CPHS*

Striking opal at Twelve Mile

We went back to Twelve Mile and a lot of people was working there, camped there. Jack Crombie went past there, Coober Pedy Jimmy; old friends like that. We lived our life here all the time see. They not thinking going anywhere long way, travelling other countries, settling down.

Sometimes when they say there's a big opal find, I go and watch whitefellas throw it out. And we sit down at the opal (noodling). Bags full, you know. We sell it and get the money and share it back. Tucker all the time, drum of water. All the water come — might be eight drums there. They come and fill 'em up. Yes, every week. Yes, and a wagon load of wood. My husband brought that load.

My husband had his own claim, big money claim but he didn't understand to work it. Probably some people robbing him. Joe's father was there looking in the holes to see if he could find big pieces, big pockets of opal. And he went back again after work again one day and he said, 'Okay. Opal might be there!' And he threw the crowbar and it stuck into the ground and hit dirt. That crowbar stuck there. Anyway, he been tell one of my brother-in-laws, Tommy Brown, 'Dig there!' And he said, 'right, don't leave it 'til morning!' (Husband was giving them the chance to throw the crowbar.) But they left it and he dug it himself. Only my husband go back to camp, get the crowbar, shovel and pick and he dug it down he did, Joe's father.

'There must be opal up here if they're digging up there.'

And he get a big opal out then, chucking it with the shovel. '*Ai!*' And we all sat down, right around, all the A<u>n</u>angu. That was the first one there, laying there, big one and he dug it down getting it all the time. All the time then, he made big money. Big money, he did. We could have bought a house. He bought a truck.

The olden time opal buyers

Not much good buyers here now. Only the old ones here in the dugouts living, you know here and they sitting down, old mens sitting down. But they good buyers, those olden time fellas and they know the opal. They can class 'em, they can weigh it and like that. They used to do that. We knew that part, you know, and today, they just anyway do things. Robbing people.

5. Settling down: Going for opal

Lennon family, c.1949
Jessie and Barney Lennon with baby Emily and three-year-old Bernard. The photograph, by the surveyor Len Beadell, was taken in Port Augusta. Bernard is watching some horses coming towards them. *Photograph: Len Beadell; Aboriginal Heritage, DOSAA*

CHAPTER 6

Displaced: 'The bomb caught us'

The bomb caught us then at Twelve Mile

The bomb caught us then. We living there, Twelve Mile all the time. We use to live out there for a long time — go in to Coober Pedy for food and water. Edna and Willie Williams were there and their two little girls, Shirley and Maureen.

The bomb been coming then. And they **knew** that — when the bomb been going to go off. They knew — the womens and mens and all. My husband and Willie and them were going into Coober Pedy all the time to get *mai* — food. They must have heard about the bomb. They didn't want to leave that mine — opals. They heard about the bomb — the mans there talking about it, all the people. But they didn't know which way it was going. They thought nothing was going to happen to us.

And me — I was home there; home all the time. Had my tent there, shed there; tanks, drums of water and the washing things. It was just coming on summer. I'm sitting home, not worrying about what's going on. I was just outside, young and healthy, looking after the little ones, Beaver ...

I siphoned the water out of the drum and I saw this shadow go past and I looked up. What was that shadow?

And it started to look hazy ...

6. Displaced: 'The bomb caught us'

British nuclear testing in Australia
3 October 1952, Monte Bello Islands; 15, 27 October 1953, Emu Junction; 16 May, 19 June 1956, Monte Bello Islands; 27 September (pictured), 4, 11, 22 October 1956, 14, 25 September, 9 October 1957, Maralinga at seven different sites.
  'Minor' trials — 1953, 1954, 1956, 1957, 1958, 1959, 1960, 1961, 1963 including the plutonium–239 deposited in the 1959 trials. *Photograph: Department of Defence; NAA*

Something's wrong!

They took a long time to come, husband and Willie Williams.

Going for opal, the mans, they seen that bomb. Right the way on that other part — west — they seen 'em. On top of the hill — they looked the bomb way. They didn't know. Smoke laying along, laying across; smoke and bluish smoke.

And the mans came back, 'Something **wrong!**' Headaches, hands over their head. Smoke and bluish smoke rolled over, come over us from *wilu̱rara* — west — the mist was coming from Mabel Creek way. Came in — filled up the hills, the holes — rolled in along the ground — to the tree tops and go around then and follow the creek. Right over the top of us — cloud we can see, like a haze. Could see their **shadows**; it was different to me.

Got the bars, crowbars, you know, shovels, picks.

Pika! — Sick!

'Come on then! We go! What are we staying here for? I think I'll pack up,' he said.

Husband had a truck, an old red Bedford.

Take the children. We had Bernard, Emily and Beaver (Stanley was a baby then at Umeewarra) — take the children to Port Augusta. Molly Brown had a baby out from Coober Pedy, Molly Brown, my sister. She brought the little one to hospital.

Yes, at Twelve Mile, the bomb came right through there — Mabel Creek. My daughter was there then. We were all picking it up, that sickness.

6. Displaced: 'The bomb caught us'

British atomic test — Emu site
In 1952, the surveyor Len Beadell was summoned from Woomera, 480 kilometres away, to the headquarters of the Long Range Weapons establishment in Adelaide to be informed in a meeting of 'top secrecy' that 'it has been decided to detonate an atomic bomb in Australia'. The site was required to be 'in an area roughly three hundred miles from Woomera in a place where radiation would not interfere with the future missile range work'.

This meeting took place almost a year before the official announcement was made. Emu was the name given to the site chosen by Beadell — a 1.5 kilometre long hard clay pan, 280 kilometres north-west of Coober Pedy. Totem I was detonated on October 15, 1953 and it was this explosion that was proved, in the eventual Royal Commission into the British Nuclear Tests, to be the creator of the 'Black Mist' so destructive to the health of the Aboriginal people at Wallatina and other places. Working from the birth dates of the children in the families involved, it was also this explosion which caused the sickness to the Lennons, Williams and others at Twelve Mile and also to those at Mabel Creek.
Photograph: Joe Kennedy; CPHS

After the bomb — moving off

To Anna Creek

We're sick then and we're going away to live somewhere better than when the bomb went off here. We're frightened. We went to Anna Creek. I forget how we got there. We went and stayed there, Anna Creek; went and lived there with the people. Old people was a stranger to us — never seen us for a long time but they know our mothers and fathers. Kampakuta — Eileen Brown, was there, her and her husband — *wati kuri palumpa*. They both was good people, you know. They found out who we was. The man knew my old husband — he was relation to him. Me and her went for rabbit — she was young and I was young. Plenty of rabbit was there — *kuka* — meat. We're feeding on rabbits there; we were allowed to eat them.

I was carrying another one; the one I lost. I lost him when he was a big fella here in Coober Pedy. I'd like to know how that went on. I feel sorry and sad to think about it now. He said, 'Mum, I'm going to the hospital.'

Doctor kept him there. I didn't know then it was that bad.

Yes, I was carrying for him then at Anna Creek.

And Finniss Springs

After Anna Creek, we went on to Finniss Springs then. Three of the kids were going to school — Beaver, Emily and Bernard.

My old man had a little job there in Finniss — not right in Finniss. He was sort of camping out in the siding there. A lot of people lived in the siding — there at Alberrie Creek. That was the name of the siding.

Work was right there at the station; he had the fencing with one of the men, one of the workers, Peter Kantassi.

6. Displaced: 'The bomb caught us'

Finniss Springs Mission revisited
Jessie Lennon's son was born in November, 1953. The family, having fled to Port Augusta Hospital in the wake of the Emu atomic bomb explosion of October 1953, arrived in Finniss Springs Mission en route from Anna Creek, just eight years after the young couple's first visit on their epic 'honeymoon' journey. By now the UAM mission was well established as this 1948 photograph of the mission buildings shows. The buildings included the mission house, hospital, store, church, motor garage, salt well windmills and Mr Warren's home and sheds. The people's camp was to the left of the photograph. A lack of water, however, continued to be a problem. *Photograph: R. Pearce, UAM; AIATSIS*

The baby's coming

Then he was working at the mine at Leigh Creek and Altman (he was the boss). Altman took him to Queensland. He went for a trip you know to get a motor car and give it to him too, to Bernard's father.

'No, baby's coming soon,' he said to me. 'No, you fellas go to Port Augusta and stop up there.'

So he sent me to Port Augusta to have the baby. I went to Port Augusta — took Emily and Beaver. He put us on the train and went back to Leigh Creek. He took Bernard to Queensland.

When I had this one, you know, I come right back. The father was home there at Alberrie Creek, home at the Finniss Springs Siding, sitting around there in the camp. I rang up the Finniss Springs Mission for him to hear about it and if he got back. He did and he got that message and he rang back and said to the mission, to Umeewarra — he said, 'I'll be waiting at the train stop and tell them I'll be coming up there.'

And he was right up at the train stop.

Yes, we'd stayed there at Umeewarra Mission. We were cleaning up then. I was washing clothes and packing up. I was happy to go back.

And he went there to the siding. My little girl (a big woman now), Emily — she was sitting on the window side when the train came in, looking out. 'Oh Dad! Oh Mum, Mum — look! Dad — Dad over there!'

And he grabbed the little one who was there, through the window, loving him up.

Yeah! We seen the motor car. Everybody always there, standing around. And all the A<u>n</u>angus — Aboriginal people too — *kungkas* — women and all. They're our people again. They good people. They're gone now. That's the first lot of people. They 'lation to us too — 'lation. Nancy Warren was there too. She was young then. She was at that siding too. She was cooking too — for Bernard and this other girl too — old Muntia, they call her. She was old granny to me. Old Molly.

6. Displaced: 'The bomb caught us'

The Ghan
The Ghan was meant to be part of the across-the-continent railway line from Port Augusta to Darwin — back in 1880! Built in stages, it eventually reached Hergott Springs (Marree) in 1883. Construction of the section to Oodnadatta became a government unemployment relief measure, providing employment for hundreds of Adelaide's jobless men. From 1891, Oodnadatta remained head of the line for the next thirty-eight years. From there freight was loaded onto the camel trains of the Afghan cameleers to go the next 293 miles to Alice Springs. The Australian Government took over the line in 1925, and because of increasing popular pressure regarding an Adelaide–Darwin service, extended the railway to Alice Springs by 1929. This followed the route of the camel trains. Previously known as the Afghan Express, shortened to the Ghan, with sleeping and dining cars it became the 'Flash' Ghan.

Flooding, problems with length of route and with mixed widths of the line gauges finally led to the completely new, shorter track being built far to the west. Opened in 1981, it runs more directly north — from Tarcoola to Alice Springs. Construction of the Alice Springs–Darwin line began in 2001 and were completed in 2004. *Photograph: R. Pearce; AIATSIS*

I'm the one that know this country!

At home with the sweet bush tucker

We were camping there at Alberrie Creek. Big dam and big trees right around. Big lot of gum trees there too; 'lollies' — gum trees got a lot of lollies.

Yes, you know I've been walking around *kutju* — by myself walking about and I been thinking — 'What kind of trees there — all shiny things sitting on the top.'

But — gum, that was; you allowed to eat that. Lot of womans — them mob — Arabana womens — been tell me too, 'Hey, we like them things on the tree there!' They were grabbing it for the kids then. It's growing on the tree — might be laying across there. They call it *tjau*. They already got a name for it — *tjau*.

We were having a good old feed all the times: bullock meat. We were eating a lot of rabbit again; *kuka palya* — good meat — they were fat!

But then we were getting worried. When the kids jump on the tree, just like they're going to take a dive in the big deep dam there, I call out to my old man, 'I'll take them back to another country! We don't want to get our kids drowned!'

6. Displaced: 'The bomb caught us'

Market day at Finniss Springs — Government rations
With the coming of white settlement in the various areas of South Australia, Aboriginal people were blocked from their former free access to country and their own food supplies. In recognition of this, government rations were distributed at selected points including mission stations and in the pastoral lease country, often at stations. In 1906 there were 42 ration stations, including 20 run by the police and 16 under station managers.

Unfortunately the food provided was nowhere near as healthy as game and bush tucker. In 1949, the South Australian Protector of Aborigines, Mr Penhall, replying to criticisms, cited that the rations available at Ooldea were — flour, tea, sugar, rice, sago, salt, potatoes, split peas and other foods, also soap, cooking utensils, blankets and tobacco (Mattingley and Hampton 1988). *Photograph: R. Pearce; AIATSIS*

Andamooka

We went to Andamooka after that. We liked it there. They was getting money there for opal. My old man worked there too in the diggings, getting opal; all that. We lived there — home. Edna Williams was there. Willie Williams was there. They were young — well, not really young; they had Shirley and Maureen and Jenny, Pauline, I think and Tjungkina — Raelene. Edna's father and mother was there — Mickey Fatt and old Bamilya. Billy Lennon mob again. All of us were there then; all the Kingoonya mob. We forgot about Coober Pedy — what Coober Pedy was like, then.

All my brothers — they was coming up and they was working around Andamooka and the stations — Arkoona, all them stations. That was good. But they were starting to have girlfriends. Emily Austin was in Umeewarra Mission then and my brother and another fella was chasing her too.

Rocky Mungeranie's mother, my sister, been come there too. They had two boys — the first brother, *ngaltutjara* — poor thing and Rocky. Rocky was a small kid, just walking 'round and his brother, he's playing around, climbing up the trees; all the pine trees there in Andamooka, you know.

He'd stand, he'd get up there and he could see the road coming; he could see the road from Port Augusta way, you know. He's looking out for the mail truck.

'The mail truck is coming now!' He's telling his mum and dad.

'Let 'im come!' his father say. 'Jump off — before you get the leg broken!'

Yes, his father growling and my sister sitting under the tree, big wattle tree. That's all we got for shelter that time. They could have worked and made a brush shelter, I suppose. They made a *kanku* — traditional shelter — all right and tent. Oh, we been in that *kanku* and tent. Big fire burning outside on the ground.

6. Displaced: 'The bomb caught us'

Andamooka
Opal was discovered at Andamooka in the early 1930s. In 1932, there were said to be eight men living there, just one with his family. According to one of them, Wally Hancock, there were also 'many others who came and went'.

The school was built by the miners in 1946 from the pines in the scrub and the minimum number of 12 students was just reached for it to be officially opened in 1947. At the end of 1948, about five years before the Lennon family arrived, the radio telephone was installed in the dugout of Mrs Rose Brooks and the Flying Doctor came from Broken Hill for the first visit. In the early 1950s, the hospital was built. Barney Lennon built his family house here in about 1956, partly above ground, partly dugout into the hill. By 1963, when the photograph was taken, above ground housing had taken hold. Opal continues to be mined today.
Photograph: Andrew Abbie; AIATSIS

I'm the one that know this country!

Joe's birth and back to Andamooka

I been going to Port Augusta **again.** I been going for Joe then. I been carrying him. All the 'nother lot was home. I took some of my childrens. Bernard stopped with his father. The father took us in the motor car to Pimba.

There's a bud car[1] they call it. The bud car was going through to Tarcoola, then going straight through to Port Augusta. It come to Pimba. It come there — stopped. We jumped on that. That was our car — the old bud car. Beaver and Bernard — they were little kids — trying to go out there by the door. It was dangerous! I tell them, 'Go back!'

When I had Joe, somebody must have brought us back. It might have been my brother — he was going with Emily Austin and she was at Umeewarra Mission. Anyway, I can see it — when I jump off that morning at Andamooka, I had a baby in my hands and I walked in the dugout and his father and Bernard was sitting in the dugout. I came in, baby in my hands and the father get it off me then and he nursing it.

That was Joe.

Everything was *palya* — good, really good, that time.

1. A fast diesel rail car used in northern South Australia to get from small settlements to main railway lines.

6. Displaced: 'The bomb caught us'

Umeewarra Mission
By the 1930s groups of Aboriginal people had moved into Port Augusta and were living in the sandhills on the edge of town. Miss Tatlock Brown who had lived among them there asked for a reserve to be built. A 200 acre (80 hectare) reserve was granted. In 1937 the Open Brethren Assemblies of South Australia established a mission there, three kilometres north of the town. It was given the traditional name of the area: Umeewarra, next to the Lake Umeewarra which remains an important site in Aboriginal life today. Pictured is the first children's home which was built over its dirt floor. Besides those who were living there, over the years, there were many other people like Jessie Lennon coming in from the north and west for hospital treatment who used the reserve as a base. *Photograph: Mrs Ivy McWilliams*

Everyone mixed in at Andamooka

At Andamooka, there was all of us there and all the young ones what them old people been have. And old Eva Cassidy too; Eva Strangways her name was. She was married to a Cassidy afterwards. They were finishing off then; they were passing away sometimes.

Lot of whitefellas there too at Andamooka. A lot of girls and womens. They good people too — happy. We go out to the dam that was full that time.

A̲nangus — Aboriginal people — they mix up with white girls, white mans. They stopped there — going to have a party by the dam. All the yabbies was there — the yabbies are still there now. We go for a party out. Eva Strangways, nice woman, had a big fire going for the cooking. We're eating *kuka ma̱lu* — eating kangaroo. I like the shoulder part — the leg's got too much meat. I like the *nyu̱ntjun̲* — the marrow; you see the old ladies break up the bone and eat the inside.

Yes and that time we didn't know where we'd be, you know — husband and me. We sort of got moved around and 'round then. We thought about coming back here to Coober Pedy then.

Drifting away from one another

Joe's father, he split up and went over to Port Augusta, sitting around there — he must have seen someone there, you know, that would have made him say to me, 'Oh, you must let me go for a month or two, you know. I can stay away — stop with the people — learn some more things, you know.'

I was thinking, '*Ai!* — that's new to talk like that!'

I was thinking, 'Oh, it's spoilt now.' We were drifting away from one another.

Then he went back here to Coober Pedy.

Me and the kids were sitting down with my mother then, at Port Augusta.

6. Displaced: 'The bomb caught us'

Umeewarra Mission, Davenport Reserve
In 1950 there were 100 people in the mission, 60 of whom were children — 36 in the home and the rest with their parents on the reserve. In 1963, the mission was renamed Davenport Reserve. In 1967, Davenport became self-governing by an elected body, the Davenport Community Council. At this time there were still 70 children in the home which continued as a separate entity. Mr Alan and Mrs Ivy McWilliams (Mr and Mrs Mac) had arrived in 1959, a few years after Miss Morton and, together with Miss Cantle, all remained at Umeewarra for over 30 years. Mr and Mrs Mac's duties included giving out the rations, and managing the dispensary next door to the ration shed, (pictured). *Photograph: Mrs Ivy McWilliams*

CHAPTER 7

Drifting: 'Everything went funny then'

Me and the kids at Port Augusta

Me and the kids were at Port Augusta — next door to Sydie and Tillie Waye. I had a job in the early part of it. I was working at Umeewarra Mission, just doing the rations for the camp mob — the A̱nangu camp. All the A̱nangu were camping around the sandhills in Port Augusta. No houses was there in that time — no houses. Only a little tin hut was there, somewhere for to give the rations.

I'm doing nothing in the day, just waiting around for the children after school. They're playing in the sandhills then and I'm giving the bread out — might be 6 o'clock.

Rations — all the fresh things, they'd give at 12 o'clock on the Friday. The mob'd come in and I'd had bread and meat and potatoes and onions and all those things; Weetbix and milk and that, you know. That was good! I was working and the kids, they were learning the kids there.

Umeewarra Mission School

They were learning the kids at Umeewarra Mission School. Old Miss Simmons was the Boss; Miss Cantle was the school teacher, poor old things. I was right there when I see all of them went away. Miss Cantle was getting an old woman — sitting back there in the chair, waving away! Poor old Miss Cantle. There was one there walking around and that was Miss Morton.

The McWilliams at Umeewarra

Then Mr Mac came there too and made it right. Mr Mac was looking after the kids there too, all the boys and girls. Mr Mac's got a lot of work for them. But he takes them out too — for *kuka* — to hunt for meat. They go camping out, eating what they wanted — what they wanted to kill: *kaltas* — sleepy lizards, *mi̱lpa̱li* — goanna. Them kids.

7. Drifiting: 'Everything went funny then'

Umeewarra / Davenport Community
This photograph of Jessie, Beaver, Billy Luke and Stanley Lennon at Umeewarra Mission was taken about 1955, when the family was visiting Stanley. With a change in Australian Government policies away from institutionalisation, the numbers of the children in the home gradually decreased at Umeewarra. Church activities continued. Mr and Mrs Mac stayed on until 1995 when Umeewarra Home former residents, now grown up and scattered throughout the state, were invited to return and help decide its future. Decisions made included turning the large dining room into the Umeewarra House Museum, while Davenport Community bought and improved the other old buildings for those past residents who wanted to go back and live in the old home. *Photograph: Mrs Ivy McWilliams*

The kids were doing well

The boys, they go up that Mount Brown Hill. They have fun up there too. My kids went; the smaller ones like Beaver went down the bottom, Bernard went half way up. And they go to Spear Creek; that's where they kill the *kalta* — the sleepy lizard; girls and boys.

Mr Mac take them for holidays too. They were doing well there, you know. They were with me. I had the house — not allowed to go outside the house. Then their father, he took Bernard away. Bernard was working with him too. Later — he tried to get the whole lot ...

Everything went funny

It was Weightman (of 'The Welfare'), you know, I don't know what his first name was — Weightman — he stopped my kids, you know. He came and take my kids to Coober Pedy.

I sort of let them go to stay where the father can get tuckers for them. If I had've stuck to my job back at Umeewarra that was given to me ... I took my own self out of the house where I shouldn't at all. I'm sorry about that too. A lot of people was going wrong ways.

The childrens' father, he looked after them then, him and that woman he lost later, the sick woman. She had cancer, I think. I had Beaver all the time. I come on the truck — mail truck to Coober Pedy, me and Beaver. Then we went back again. He wanted to stop with me. After that, he wanted to take him again — send him to school here.

Oh, everything went funny then ...

7. Drifiting: 'Everything went funny then'

Barney and Dorothy Lennon
Over the years, Barney Lennon (Jessie Lennon's first husband) and his wife Dorothy were temporary and long-term carers for a number of Aboriginal children as well as their own. In this photograph — taken about 1970 when they lived near the school — Joe (Jessie's son) is first on the right. Barney and Dorothy were well-known identities in Coober Pedy and committed members of the Lutheran Church. Both were members of Umoona Council, the Aboriginal Council which was elected by Aboriginal residents of Coober Pedy in 1975 to take over from the Government.

As in the early days, Barney Lennon continued to mine for opal and he had many other contract jobs in the district. Later he worked for WOMA, alcohol prevention and rehabilitation, while Dorothy was a health worker. The Lennons continued to be a strong presence in the community for many years. *Photograph: Lutheran Archives*

I'm the one that know this country!

Judy's father

I saw him then, my daughter Judy's father — Leo Strangways. We was at Andamooka all the time. We were going with one another then, you know, like loving one another there. Judy was born that time then.

Judy called herself Strangways and everything just like him — face, you know, just like Leo. He went and seen it in the hospital. He wanted to see the baby all the time. He wanted to find out that 'This is mine.' He wanted to know. And he went and seen it in the hospital. It looked like him. He went home then.

I been bring Judy out from the hospital; I been come out, you know. He **liked** his kid too, you know.

And thinking about it, I got the baby, got the girl and I should have married and gone back to **Kingoonya** country. We used to all talk about that — go back to Wilgena and all them places, Bon Bon …

7. Drifiting: 'Everything went funny then'

Jessie and Judy
This photograph of Jessie and baby Judy was taken in Port Augusta in 1963. Port Augusta now has the largest Aboriginal population outside Adelaide with many people living in the town as well as in the community. The town has become an important regional area for Indigenous services. With the scaling down of important industries in the town, the general population has decreased to the extent that it is estimated that Aboriginal people make up just under 20 per cent of the town's population (Australian Bureau of Statistics 2010). The Director of the Pika Wiya Health Service, Charlie Jackson, estimates that Port Augusta has the largest Aboriginal population for a regional town in Australia, encompassing about a quarter of the town's total population in 2010. This includes a large number of people from diverse areas, speaking approximately twelve different languages. *Photograph: Mrs Ivy McWilliams*

I'm the one that know this country!

Yes, Leo Strangways and the grandmother raised Judy

I left her with the grandmother when she was small. Leo Strangways was all the time there in Port Augusta and from there he used to go out working. He went back to Coondambo Station. Judy was with the grandmother all the time then. Big camp was there at Coondambo too. Big camp; mens working, the old mans, young fellas; the old mans teaching the young fellas to go to work. That was different; it was an A̱nangu *ngura* — Aboriginal camp. Sometimes they'd go to Coober Pedy, travelling with the camel wagon

All the Strangways — old *tji̱lpi* — old man Strangways, different Strangways was there — Old Eva Strangways and she had the family. (They all scattered everywhere now; some down at Port Augusta.)

Judy's father, he got sick when I was later on here in Coober Pedy. He was sick all the time — too far gone he was, drinking the drink. The doctor told him, 'Can't you get yourself fixed up.' He might have **stopped** drinking and stayed in the hospital.

One time I saw him stopping at Judy's. Judy was married then — got kids. And I went back there, 'round there again to see Judy. And Judy said, 'Mum, you come down there. Dad's sitting around there, watching the girls, Robyn and Becca and the boy.' (Little ones, they all little ones.)

And he sit down. 'I'll watch the kids,' Judy's father say, you know.

'Hello Dad. What, you want to watch the kids? What you want to watch the kids for? You want me to get you a bottle of drink?'

Yes, Leo and the grandmother raised Judy. Eva — Eva Strangways was the grandmother and she's the best woman going. And he was a good fella, you know. He could have been still living here today — he was younger than everybody.

7. Drifiting: 'Everything went funny then'

Coondambo Station and the Strangways family
The Strangways family and their camel wagon are pictured here in 1948 at East Well on Coondambo Station where they were employed. Coondambo had a ration depot and the 'main place' on the station for Aboriginal people was the south camp.

Tim Strangways, the father of Leo, is standing to the right of the photograph, holding the horse's reins while his wife Eva, 'the best woman going', holds the camel reins. His brother, Sid Strangways, lived in Coober Pedy for many years, being a committed member of the Lutheran Church. *Photograph: Len Beadell; Aboriginal Heritage, DOSAA*

Bringing Judy up to Coober Pedy and taking her back again

One time I picked Judy up again and took her away again. Small girl she was too, walking around. I sort of took her away and never asked the grandmother. Brought her right back here, Coober Pedy and my children's father was over there and their step-mother and the children were there too — Bernard and Emily mob.

And their father, he seen my baby, seen my girl and it give him a shock too, you know.

'Oh come on here to old Daddy!' He been grab her and that 'nother little girl too, Emsie, **their** little daughter. Them two were both the same, both small girls. Them two both stayed there then — at Emsie's camp.

I camped behind Bernard's house then; that little tin house on the reserve. Bernard was married then, had children then. I took Judy back one Races Day. It was at the Kingoonya Races. And the grandmother was right there too — waiting for her. I had her for about a year.

Old father-in-law, Jim Lennon

Millie Taylor, my old sister-in-law, she and old Jim Lennon, her father, was staying in Andamooka all the time. She'd come there to Port Augusta, get some medicine and things and she'd go back. She was minding her old father, old Jim Lennon, my old father-in-law. Then she sent him down to Port Augusta.

I don't know what went wrong — he passed away, poor old thing.

7. Drifiting: 'Everything went funny then'

Umoona Reserve
Now called Umoona Community, the reserve was set aside for the exclusive use of local Aboriginal people because they had been dispossessed of their traditional lands. The reserve (approximately 2025 hectares) was established in 1959, with Pastor Fred Traeger appointed by the State Welfare Department and the Lutheran Church as administrator. His main duty as set out by the Government was to act as opal buyer and shopkeeper for the Aboriginal people. In 1975 the Aboriginal community adopted the name Umoona, which means red mulga tree, common in the area. This photograph was taken in the early days of the reserve. The houses were tin sheds with a hole in the middle for a fire. *Photograph: Joe Troester; CPHS*

Travelling to Ceduna

I didn't go back with nobody then. I didn't go back to Andamooka. I was with my sister-in-law Annie and my youngest brother, Jimmy in his motor car. We went Ceduna way — travelling around.

Coming back to Coober Pedy

I fell in love with another man too. That's Tilly Waye's brother. We come back here, Coober Pedy. We staying here again in Barney Lennon's place. Everybody camped out everywhere there — across the road from the police station — down the flats, not far from the Alice Springs Road. We all of us lived there — all the Fatts lived there. (Nobody much living I think of Fatts; only Edna Fatt — she's Edna Williams now, *kutju* — the only one.)

Then we both went travelling, we went to work at this place, Billa Kallina out from Kingoonya. They wanted a man to come and work there. We all worked there then. We like it — instead of people drunk.

But then we came back here, Coober Pedy and that man tell himself he's a good man and he go for drink. He go altogether. He don't drink and chase womans. He just go and these things happen to him. Yes. And I have to hear about it and I say, 'Hey — next time you go again — Go!'

And I just left him alone then.

Just went like that then. Me and Putitja's mother — Patricia Fatt's mother — her mother was a good friend to me. Me and her — just two sisters, just like we are — her mother was my cousin. Oh and we travelled about and mixed up with the people who were drinking.

7. Drifiting: 'Everything went funny then'

Ceduna — The Eyre Highway
It was not until 29 September 1976, after many years of political pressure by Western Australia on the Australian Government, that the final section of the Eyre Highway was sealed. As a result the traffic doubled.

Up until World War II there were not even surveyed roads west of Penong — old stock tracks were still in use. In 1941, due to fears of invasion, huge efforts achieved a graded road from Penong to the Western Australia border — 485 kilometres in six months. Western Australia completed its section by 1969 and the Port Augusta–Ceduna section was already sealed by 1964. *Photograph: Andrew Abbie; AIATSIS*

I'm the one that know this country!

Something goes wrong

I had the baby for Clem Lennon then — Millie Taylor and Tillie Waye's brother. Something went wrong. They took me to Ceduna — flew me down to have him. The baby was making me sick. They took me to the plane, me and another lady, white woman.

I had the baby. It was too small. It was a little boy — Clem Michael, *ngal<u>t</u>u* — poor thing; good little baby too. He's just like his father too. They couldn't do nothing — the doctors. Oh, those nurses, they been telling me, 'Oh, you shouldn't have had this baby at all! You shouldn't have had him at all. That should still be in **there!**'

And they been touch my *tjuni* — my stomach.

It came too early, I suppose. If they had one of those cribs [humidicrib] down there — I've seen babies like that again; they been grow them up. That woman, woman doctor — she been take his photo. 'We'll get it big and you'll have his photo,' she been telling me. And I never went back to that woman doctor, you know, Christian woman she was.

Never mind.

7. Drifiting: 'Everything went funny then'

The flying medical services
This photograph, taken in May 1963, shows outpatients, including Maudie Brown (right) awaiting the flying doctor at Coober Pedy's Aboriginal Reserve, where the CDEP office is today.

In 1938 the Bush Church Association (BCA) Flying Medical Services based in Ceduna had been declared open. From the mid-1950s to mid-1960s, Dr Merna Mueller was the only doctor in the far west and north, including Coober Pedy where, as she described in 1998, 'the population sometimes reached a thousand and many transcontinental railway towns each with about hundred people'; also Yalata Aboriginal Community and station properties. In 1965 (just three months after she delivered Jessie Lennon's premature baby) she was awarded the OBE. In 1968 Flying Medical Service handed over to the 'better equipped and better financed Royal Flying Doctor Service at Port Augusta'. This service continues today. *Photograph: Andrew Abbie; AIATSIS*

A ride back all the way to Coober Pedy

I came back up here again. I know the kids was here. Only for the kids I come back. Yes. I got a ride back there again in the plane to Kingoonya; one lady was coming back there again. I got a ride to Kingoonya!

And we were all wanting to get a ride then from Kingoonya on Jacob's truck, mail truck, the Coober Pedy mail truck. But he had too much load. But a motor car came — Mickey Reid's (Ngingil Reid's father) mob and give us a ride.

'You want to wait there, girl, and I'll give you a ride,' he said. Then half way he broke down — at Peake Station. Something snapped off.

I was just going to have a sleep, you know, on the road there and thinking of how I got to go and then, oh — Ngingil was saying, 'Dad's going to get a ride for you too!'

I see a whitefella's motor car coming then. This old *tjilpi*, old man, been telling me then to get a ride — the old minister been come from Ceduna way; Lutheran fellow, Pastor Eckermann. He give me a ride — he's too good, you know. I was happy, sitting along, eating pie, biscuits.

He's talking all the way with me.

People living everyway

As soon as we got back to Coober Pedy here, everyone asleep here in car bodies. Lot of car bodies was everyway. Just anyway chuck a mattress — 'round near the shop, on the Flat — Anangu *tjuta* — all the Aboriginal people. Then lately they find out they can have a house.

Bernard and his old wife — first wife — had a house there at Umoona — on the Reserve there. Beaver was a Sunday School preacher working with Pastor Kreiger — that young fella preacher with no kids.

7. Drifiting: 'Everything went funny then'

The Lutherans
Jessie's son Beaver is pictured here standing in the back row, third from right, next to Mr Grieger. Next to them are Peggy and Ronny Brown and Monty O'Toole. They were all part of this Lutheran congregation in the 1960s. In 1964, the building in the background was dedicated as the Lutheran Aboriginal Mission Church Hall, and was served by Pastor Traeger. The 1965 church records state there were '246 souls under spiritual care, mixed Natives and whites, with 60 Sunday School pupils'. Pastor Traeger fought to establish a school for the Aboriginal children, which was initially opposed by the State Education Department. The school was initially held in the community hall in 1960. *Photograph: Lutheran Archives*

CHAPTER 8

Going home: 'I got sick over the bomb'

Opal!

I've been all the time here then — going out for opal. Yes, many years I was going out for opal. We'd go out from here, Coober Pedy — camp at Twelve Mile, you know; going out all the time from there again, noodling. I was with Bernard all the time, Bernard and his wife, his old wife. We used to go for opal every day.

They had children all there with them. Go to school; send them to school; bring them back; sometimes leave them with somebody, might be with the brother-in-law, George Cooley, in the house somewhere in town; go out back to work only with the little ones.

Yes, in the morning we'd always be waiting for the man to come and work on the opal and chuck the dirt out. We camp there. We got our own fires there, wood fires. We don't camp right at the working ground. We're camping a long way away. Bush might be there. Brush — we break up that brush to make a wind break for the night.

Lot of another visitors would come. They found out about the opal. They found out Barney Lennon was a good opal digger — at Eight Mile and then shifted away to Twelve Mile.

8. Going home: 'I got sick over the bomb'

Shopping days
Mail and shopping day have always been important events in the lives of Coober Pedians. During the 1950s and 1960s, Jack and Edna Brewster ran their store, which included a boarding house. On shopping days, many Aboriginal people would shop together using scarce transport

This photograph shows people organising their stores on a truck — thought to be owned by Andrew Kiltie's father — parked near Brewster's store (at the intersection of the old Alice Springs Road). According to Eileen Wingfield (Jessie's niece), the kangaroo dog in the foreground belonged to Tottie Bryant. She had the only kangaroo dog in Coober Pedy for many years. The child standing facing the camera is Warwick Jones. *Photograph: Wayne Zanker*

Noodling on the dumps

The mans — the opal miners working down there below all the time throwing the dirt out — the dirt what they don't like. Machine is sending it out, down the bottom there — the blower bringing it up. They work with a machine. When the good opal there, they're chucking it out and nobody there up top to grab that opal — gets lost in the second dirt covering it up again. And you can't see it. You'd have to dig down deep again. Like that.

We use to always go noodling and we'd get a bag full! We sit up on the dump and dig around. Scratch around, scratching the stones and sand any way. Get 'em, get the opal. Go back and put it in the bottle, pour in the water and leave it there — soak. We look at it there. It might be dirty still — got that dirty dust. It's a little bit of rock. Then they file it up, you know with a file and then the dirt come off. The dust get in your eye too!

One time it was all **red** and **green** and it might be **red-grey** and all that. It might be the old grey too. They cut that all out — class it, put the red-grey to one side and put the second grey class to one side again.

Yes, you put the opal in the jar, clean it up — soak it first and rinse it out nice and clean. Big colour shining from a long way! Just put it in the jar again, put fresh water, nice and clean. Put the top on the jar and look at it! Have a look!

'How much I'm going to get for this.'

And 'nother people, another lot of boys — they know how much. Bernard will be saying, 'You'll get money for this.' Bernard's a good luck man too.

We're all just happy. The kids find opal too, you know …

8. Going home: 'I got sick over the bomb'

Noodling on the dumps
Noodling (picking through the mullock heaps for opal) was a good money earner for many people on the opal fields. As mechanisation of mining grew, especially in the 1960s, so did noodling for the bits of opal that were inadvertently discarded in the dirt sent to the top. Ultimately, however, mechanisation brought about the invention of noodling machines, which now compete with hand noodlers. Aboriginal people today continue to 'go out for opal'. *Photograph: Isobel White; AIATSIS*

I'm the one that know this country!

Selling the opal

We been go and give it to the boys to sell it. I'll give it to Bernard. Bernard takes it, class it, get the price on it. The mens here be buying it in the town here. They know which fellas is the good buyers. They take it there — to their houses. Those mens like to cut it down, you know. Might be $2000, you know, like that they might ask it to the buyer.

And one might be saying, 'No.'

Ask for another one — 'Oh go and try this other fella,' he say. 'If you can't get that much, well, you come back here and show it to us.'

They go on like that all the time 'til they get it and buy it.

And the seller — he's selling it; that's his opal. He wants that money — right money. He'll go 'til he get that right money.

Yes!

That might be Bernard selling it. And he'd say, 'No, I'm not selling yet.'

They'll chase you back — to your house — when they want it.

They're only trying to — **bluff.** Yes — bluff.

I know the trouble always goes on when they try to sell it, you know. They try to cut you off — cut your word off. You might be asking for that big price, asking for the right price. They look at it and run **away!** You go and sit down home — dreaming. And still they like it. Come back and offer you. You might say, 'No.' Bernard might say, 'No. Only that first offer I put there.'

'No, you're too hard,' they might say.

But if they want it, they'll take it.

8. Going home: 'I got sick over the bomb'

Coober Pedy in 1967
The lower main street of Coober Pedy in 1967 was a barely defined gibber-strewn dirt track. Individual wind-driven generators, called free-lights, are visible as there was no town power. The large corrugated iron building was the three-year-old Lutheran Aboriginal Mission Church. In the 1960s the mechanisation of opal mining created a boom in the industry. Many men, including a high proportion of European immigrants, saw this as a chance to get rich on their own initiative. Greeks, Italians, Croatians and Serbs, followed by Chinese opal buyers, were the largest migrant groups, but many other nationalities came as well. Population growth forced development; a new hospital, the first school, and another (underground) church. *Photograph: Traeger family; CPHS*

I'm the one that know this country!

Getting out the opal with dynamite

Four Mile and all those places along the Mabel Creek Road used to be good places for opal — the diggings all along this side there. All left behind now.

They used to get the opal out with dynamite. That dirt fall out and they just chuck it away again. That's where the opal come out too and they miss it — they miss the opal. Lucky ones sitting up the top when they get it. My boys been doing a lot of good time like that; all my boys — Bernard, Stanley, Beaver too, Joe. They were tough. They can't say that they didn't get opal. They got it the same time as the miner got it.

They didn't tell one another they get it. They just pick it up and lick to see the colour. Never think about it that that dynamite dirt would give them a headache too. Some people suffer with headache. I know that's all through dynamite dirt that they licking. They lick it and spit on it to see the nice colour and dynamite dirt get on their tongue. They forget themselves and get a headache then.

Yes, money there that time. There was opal — real money that time when we go. Cut the work off and stay there. Sometimes we find it and have our parties there.

They could have been rich.

They buy a motor car.

'Plenty more times,' we all think. But plenty more time gone past.

8. Going home: 'I got sick over the bomb'

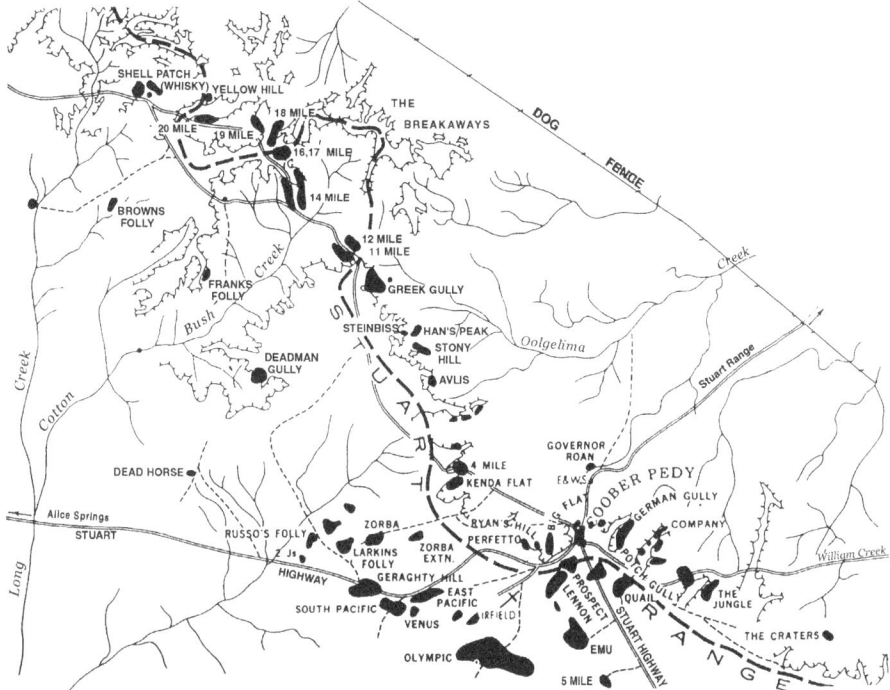

The opal field in 1980
By 1980, the Coober Pedy opal fields had developed extensively along the Stuart Range escarpment to become the largest producer of opal in the world. *Map: Adapted with permission from a map supplied by PIRSA*

The Coober Pedy opal field is 4000 square kilometres with each miner holding a claim by 50 metres by 50 metres or 100 metres by 150 metres. There are 253 registered miners with many more associates (people who may not do the actual mining). The Precious Stone Field as it is called, stretches from the township of Coober Pedy to 57.4 kilometres south and 53.5 kilometres north. The other boundaries are defined by roads, stretching 19 kilometres to Oodnadatta Road, 32 kilometres south-south-west along the Manguri Road (crossing the Adelaide to Darwin railtrack), and 27.2 kilometres along the William Creek Road.

I got sick over the bomb

I got sick over the bomb. I got cancer.

I been go away. Long time.

I used to go to different towns and I often got sick. We went to Hawker and I was in the hospital there. Some ladies look after us — in a tent there we were living.

And come back here Coober Pedy and after that I was getting it then.

I don't know nothing about that sickness. And this woman here, you know, Sister Vicki — she was asking that doctor, specialist, you know, to come to see; to come to see the womans here — what they might get it.

Yes, I don't know nothing about that sickness. I was still going walking and digging for opal and Sister Vicki told me. She called me over — tell me. I went right ahead with it. They got it out — operation.

She tell another lot too. That 'nother lot was good womans too, you know. They should have hurried up and say to them. Those womans had it the wrong way, they said it the wrong way 'round. They said, 'We're not old enough to get **that!** *Nganana* — we — we're too young! It can't be like this.'

Ngaltutjara! Poor things! They lost their life. They don't know what was coming to them. *Ngurpa* — they were ignorant of these things.

They were asking about the sickness. Yes, and I been tell 'em too.

'*Ai! — pika!* Oh, you're sick.

Doctoraku wangkaku. Go and talk to the doctor. You fellas get in there and show yourselves, you know. That's what the doctor wants to know — if you fellas have got it or not.'

8. Going home: 'I got sick over the bomb'

W.B. MacDougall and the British nuclear tests
'Mr MacDougall,' said H.B. (name under taboo) at Yalata in 1992, 'was a tall one. Red hair, broken hand. Talked Pitjantjatjara. A good fella. Came to Ooldea in a 4WD — Jeep. He stopped over there at Woomera — that was his *ngura* — his home. He came over here, went to Cundalee [WA].
Go and have a look — everywhere.'

Walter MacDougall was one of the two Patrol Officers in South Australia during the period of the British nuclear testing. From 1955 he was also given authority in Western Australia where this photograph was taken. The two men had the impossible task of patrolling the entire area in an effort to ensure Aboriginal people stayed away from the region, as many continued to follow their traditional way of life. When Ooldea Mission closed in June 1952, MacDougall caught up with those who had elected to travel north and brought them to the new southern location at Yalata. Several times he cut rations or ordered people to move back home; people who had travelled long distances, for example from Yalata to Coober Pedy, for ceremonies. He had a good relationship with Aboriginal people but was under great pressure from the Long Range Weapons Organisation 'to clear the area'. *Photograph: Winifred Hilliard; AIATSIS*

Other good womans suffering

I've been doing that all the time — telling the other womans to go. When those cottages was opened up down there at Umoona, on the reserve there, — the little middle ones there, the tin houses with their own verandah, the two roomed houses — I came back after that that time. And that's when I saw that other woman suffering.

'*Ai!* What's wrong with her? She's crying. Take her!' They took her away. But too late.

My sister, Eileen Wingfield's mother; she was like that too. Eileen told me that.

Yes, I got my cancer out. Some of the other womans, poor things, passed away. I wasn't shamed to say about it. Mustn't get shamed.

I had the operation; they got it out, the cancer.

A long time we've been talking Maralinga, talking about the bomb

And for a long time we've been talking Maralinga. We talk about opal and when we got sick at Twelve Mile — getting opal; the same time as that smoke been go down to we-fellas then. I had a little girl, Emily then and Beaver, Bernard too. We left Coober Pedy — just through that bomb.

Meeting, meeting ... Trying for it, trying for the money, the compensation. And we get tired.

Archie Barton said the money went back the other way — Maralinga Tjarutja. That's why Archie can't say nothing much about it. Putting in the right date, right day, what the doctors say ... Papers get lost, long ago hospital papers.

8. Going home: 'I got sick over the bomb'

From Emu to Maralinga
Even before the nuclear explosions at Emu, (shown here with WWII Hurricanes on site), it was realised that that location was both too far inland and from a railway line. Beadell was directed to the south-west and in August of the next year, 1954, the Government agreed to 'the permanent test site' of Maralinga, north of Watson siding on the East–West line.

The Government revoked the Ooldea Reserve and Aboriginal people, now south at Yalata Station, west at Cundalee, Western Australia and elsewhere, were prohibited from entering their traditional areas for the next 30 years. A bitumen road was built directly north of Watson to Maralinga Village which was constructed, complete with hospital and swimming pool. The road and the village are still intact today. It was from this area that the seven remaining atomic bombs were detonated and where the even more lethal experiments with plutonium took place. Secrecy was very strict. The Maralinga Village, after many years of negotiation was handed over to the traditional owners, the southern Pitjantjatjara in 2009. *Photograph: Joe Kennedy; CPHS*

Yes, talking about the compensation

Joe was talking about his girl then, my granddaughter. His baby then that got the cancer. He was trying to straighten that out then.

'How come that Naomi got cancer, as a baby she got it?' It come through me, the grandmother. She got it all right. Another lot was like that — big mob of people

Is there someone we could ring to, or talk to, or write to? We went out to Twelve Mile with the whitefella lawyer. We went out last year with him and I done my best. And someone coming, talking about checking the motor cars and grounds, Twelve Mile — last year they were talking about it. They were coming. But now, no **money** to check it.

That's all about it. We tried and tried and can't do anything any other way.

And I'm wishing for somebody to find the right word for us and we might get it. Shouldn't be giving in, we poor things. We went through the *pika* — the sickness. We went through that bomb. Other girls there, they copped it there — the bomb.

We still think about it, we still talk about it.

8. Going home: 'I got sick over the bomb'

The Royal Commission into the British Nuclear Testing in Australia
In 1983, Yankunytjatjara man, Yami Lester was ill, home from work in Alice Springs half listening to the radio, when he heard an interview with English scientist, Sir Ernest Titterton — one of the main players in the British nuclear test series. Blind since the early 1950s and sure it was the result of nuclear fallout, Yami was astounded to hear Sir Ernest's categorical assurance that no Aboriginal people had been harmed by the series. He rang the Adelaide paper, the *Advertiser* which eventually ran a series of investigative reports. A former Maralinga serviceman, John Burke, who was in hospital dying of cancer, then told what he knew. As a result of much pressure, the Royal Commission into British Nuclear Testing was finally convened in 1985 where service personnel, white station people and Aboriginal people all gave evidence. Unfortunately, people at Coober Pedy were not involved and in the early 1990s, Jessie Lennon, her late husband, Ricky Brown and Larry Pilungu Crombie made strenuous, but unsuccessful, efforts to state their own cases on behalf of those locally affected. In 2009, the campaign for compensation restarted with the involvement of a team of English lawyers. Jessie's family have continued to be involved.

This photograph shows a bunker at the Emu bombsite, c.1960. *Photograph: Joe Kennedy; CPHS*

I'm the one that know this country!

The one I lately lost

He was always trying for it, trying for the compensation — the one I lately lost. It was him and me and Larry Crombie — we-fellas, and Edna and the others — we been trying for it. Asking for the meetings, going along …

Long time back, him and me — we first met one another in Kingoonya. But he must have seen me when I was a girl, Chapman's camp — I don't know anything …

Mother been taking us, coming up this way, up here, Coober Pedy way too, you know when old stepfather was working.

And they talk about, 'Come on this way now.' (We don't know nothing about it.) 'Get ready!'

Early days — our families on the Netting job together

We had an old truck. This old man that worked with him, old Chapman, had an old truck. Old Chapman and my old stepfather, old Bill Austin, they were partners — fencing. The Fencing — Dog Fencing — the Netting went right around. Going right around to Ingomar there. It comes to the middle here somewhere and it goes right back to behind Commonwealth Hill and right back to Mulgathing. Goes right to Tarcoola and beyond Tarcoola.

Well, my man, the one I lately lost, his father started working with him, my stepfather. He's a station fella; old Jack I think his name was. He's working at the station — Commonwealth Hill — Mulgathing.

He knows all the fencing, the father. **He's** with his father and mother too — like I was with my mother and father too — at Chapman's camp.

We're the Kingoonya mob.

8. Going home: 'I got sick over the bomb'

Main street 1976
The Coober Pedy main street (later named Hutchison Street) being traversed by a tour bus (on the right), flanked by Mick Lucas and Sons supermarket and the Opal Cave. The large supermarket subsequently burned to the ground but was immediately rebuilt. By this time residential dugouts took up most of the hillside and the Italian Club was on the top of the hill. *Photograph: Peter Caust; CPHS*

Meeting up again — Coober Pedy

Then not long ago, Coober Pedy we were just meeting up again — getting on. I didn't know how to **take** him. And I thought about it myself and I thought I should just let him go for his hospital trouble.

I was thinking that. I worried my head off. When I wanted to go somewhere he'll say, 'Come on, we'll go down to the hospital and get a medicine.' And I couldn't be saying anything to go **my** way, you know ... You've got to be going that way. But that's how sick he was. I woke up to it. I felt it myself. Well I'll just have to go the same way.

We had the house near the basketball courts first. Then we got this house. This is **our** house — our new house they made. That's why I come back to this house.

I like to sit here, live here.

And he was younger than me, you know.

He was a Tracker, you know. Only once he talked about it, talked about getting that bloke. One big word, one big story. Then — finish!

8. Going home: 'I got sick over the bomb'

Tracker Ricky Brown and the Pine Valley murder hunt
Ricky Brown was one of the five trackers involved in the 1958 famous South Australian murder hunt at Pine Valley station, north of the River Murray town of Renmark. The station boss, Mr Neville Lord had been murdered in his bed by a station hand. Every day the hunt made front page headline news in both Adelaide daily papers and featured in Max Jones' book, *Tracks*, from which this photograph is reproduced. It shows (from left) Albert Anunga, Detective Max Jones, Ricky Brown and Morgan Williams. The other trackers were Jimmy James and Daniel Moodoo; all five being originally from Ooldea. Although, according to Ricky Brown, 'it was raining, thunder and lightning — water everywhere', almost immediately they picked up the track. Continuing to search out in front with sore eyes and headaches from intense concentration in the 'hot heat', the trackers took turns in the search. Eventually Ricky Brown and Morgan Williams were sent on ahead and when they saw the tracks doubling back they knew their task was over. In Adelaide the trackers were congratulated by 'the biggest mob' and nearly 40 years later, in 1994, not long before he died, Ricky Brown (then Jessie Lennon's husband) was given an award for his services.
Photograph: Adelaide Advertiser; Max Jones

The Glendambo meeting

And I been get that motor car then — they give me that Toyota then. And we went out to these meeting people.

The meeting, Glendambo meeting, you know — he got one notice to it and thinking, 'I'll have to go this meeting then.' I said, 'No, you should leave it.'

He was laying down there and Twinkie washing the Toyota outside there. Twinkie, my big granddaughter washing that Toyota outside here, washing it for us to go. At four o'clock, we were going.

(And Emily say, 'Nevermind, Mum. He's a man that nobody can't stop from driving and going to any meetings. He like his driving and he had to go to watch that land because he's a *wati*. He was the main one left, over this side of it.')

And good all the way we went.

We went and we had plenty of good *kuka,* meat, too; plenty of tails, you know, *malu* — kangaroo — tails.

Just when we got there to Glendambo, somebody was cooking *kalaya* — emu. Oh, we had a good feed. He just went to sleep with me and — coughing. And that was the finish of it then.

He used to find a lot of opal. *Ngaltutjara!* Poor thing!

Happy together we were.

I'd like to sit down here and go the same way.

But I'm all right though, *ini?* I'm all right.

8. Going home: 'I got sick over the bomb'

Coober Pedy

In 2010, Coober Pedy and its surrounding areas had an estimated Aboriginal population of 1500, as part of a total population of about 3800 (Steve Baines 2010). Although opal mining continues, it has declined while tourism has grown in importance. Large trees now grow throughout the town and two grassed sports ovals are in use.

Coober Pedy is still known as the 'Opal Capital of the World'. The opal is still there but harder to find. Diesel, explosive's costs and registration have all risen, as has the average age of the opal miners.

Coober Pedy now has modern Council Chambers that include a Tourist Information Centre. To meet the demands of tourism, many facilities and attractions have been developed in recent years, including a four-star underground hotel with swimming pool. Underground living, opal mining, and Coober Pedy's unique, multicultural, outback character make it an attraction to visitors from all over the world. *Photograph: Michele Madigan*

CHAPTER 9
Last word: 'I'm the one who know'

Tjalyiri

I'm an old woman now — big mob of grandchildren. I'm thinking about a homelands now. We'd like to shift back to Tjalyiri now — Tallaringa. That's my mother's homelands; that's the same place where they've been travelling around. My mother told me all about those things; I'm satisfied with that — really happy.

My last word

Well this is what I want to say. We travelled from some other places and travelled back this way again.

Old people, the old *tjilpis* did that travelling themselves before they ran into the train line — before the whitefellas built that line. They had no whitefella names; only Anangu — Aboriginal — names.

We seen all them old *tjilpis* — the Old People ...

But we fellas, we came from Kingoonya to here, travelling on camels.

We're the people that have been here longer. I'm an old woman now and I been **here!** I grew up **here,** Coober Pedy! I started when I was a little girl from here. Little girl and mother brought us, me, my brothers here.

And our children — when I had Bernard, Emily, Beaver, Stanley — and Joe was nothing — oh, we sat down for a long time with the kids over here, Coober Pedy.

I'm the one who know everyway.

Ngura nyangatja ngayuku — This is my home!

9. Last word: 'I'm the one who know'

Jessie Lennon at Tjalyiri (Tallaringa), 1993. *Photograph: Fern Haines*

Epilogue

Sadly, during the production of the first edition of this book, Jessie Lennon passed away. She is survived by six children and many grandchildren and great-grandchildren. This book is for them.

While attempts have been made to decontaminate some land affected by the British nuclear tests, and compensation has been awarded to the Maralinga people and a few other individuals, the people of Coober Pedy and its immediate surrounds have received nothing. The fight continues.

The Long-lasting Legacy of Maralinga

Maggie Brady
Centre for Aboriginal Economic Policy Research,
Australian National University

From the time of the development of the Woomera rocket range in 1947, several observers had predicted that the planned rocket tests would be followed by the testing of atomic, rather than conventional, weapons.[1] Others described talk of future atomic tests as 'nonsense'. Public figures who worked with Aboriginal people, such as Dr Charles Duguid (who had founded Ernabella mission in 1937), and Dr Donald Thomson (an anthropologist), were concerned about possible atomic tests and protested against the development of the rocket range on the grounds that it would be a threat to desert Aborigines. Dr Duguid encouraged opponents of the rocket range to maintain their hostility to the plan, hoping the public would see in the proposals,

> *a final token of Australia's disregard of her minority race. Shot and poisoned as they were in the earlier days, neglected and despised more lately, must our Aborigines now be finally sacrificed and hurried to extinction by sudden contact with the mad demands of twentieth century militarism?*[2]

Thomson and Duguid were thought to be troublemakers and even 'communists' for supporting Aboriginal interests in such a public manner.

Although neither Woomera itself, nor the 'guided missiles' launched there ever became part of an atomic testing program, Duguid and Thomson were largely correct in their assumptions. Between 1953 and 1963 a region northwest of Woomera did indeed become a major testing ground for atomic weapons. Following the initial blasts at the Monte Bello islands off the Western Australian coast, Emu Field northwest of Mabel Creek station in South Australia was selected as the next testing site. After two explosions at Emu (Totem 1 and Totem 2), a more permanent test site closer to a rail link was required, and a location was found 200 kilometres to the south. It came to be known as Maralinga.

The tests at Emu and Maralinga had an immediate and long-lasting impact on hundreds of Aboriginal people living in the surrounding regions, as Jessie Lennon's personal history shows. The tests caused fear and confusion, they damaged and contaminated the desert and its rockholes and disrupted peoples' freedom of movement. The prohibition on entry to their land that lasted for thirty years undermined the cultural unity of the Pitjantjatjara, and affected peoples' attachment to sites and their religious knowledge.[3] The socio-cultural, emotional, spiritual and physical effects of the tests have persisted to the present day.

Finding Maralinga

In October 1953, the surveyor Len Beadell of the Weapons Research Establishment was sent out from Emu to search for an alternative atomic test site. The authorities had already considered Woomera itself and even Groote Eylandt as possible locations, but these had been rejected.[4] Beadell discovered a promising place 40 kms north of Ooldea, and it was relatively close to the east-west railway line, a crucial requirement for transporting supplies and equipment. It was agreed that the site was 'ideal', and a month later the location called X300 was given a new name: Maralinga, an Aboriginal term from elsewhere meaning 'thunder'. The scientists found the term in an early book of 'Aboriginal words'. There was just one problem with the new site. Maralinga was located right in the middle of the north-south route taken by Aboriginal people who followed the rockholes that linked the Musgrave Ranges around Ernabella in the north, with Ooldea Soak in the south. Ooldea Soak was known to Aboriginal people throughout the Western Desert who had visited its permanent waters for thousands of years. It was a major gathering and ceremonial place and the evidence of this is visible today, as the stone flakes of tools made by these visitors litter the dunes. It is a huge archaeological site, described by researchers as an 'ancient metropolis'.[5] Because of the water supply available from the Soak, a siding was built close to it during construction of the Transcontinental railway. Daisy Bates lived there too for sixteen years, and she was followed by missionaries of the United Aborigines Mission (UAM) who built an outpost at the Soak.

Jessie Lennon describes in her life story how she travelled as a young girl with her family to Ooldea ('Yultu') where she saw Daisy Bates' camp, and she tells how the Antikirinya and Pitjantjatjara people walked in naked from the spinifex, going for water at the Soak. Daisy Bates had lived at the Soak between 1919 and 1936, but she disapproved of missionaries and once Mr and Mrs Harrie Green of the UAM arrived, she departed. This was when rations began to be distributed regularly. In the early 1940s, drought was driving the spinifex people out of the desert, and word spread rapidly about the food available at Ooldea. Many people made trips into the mission from distant waterholes and carried flour back out into the desert so that relatives could 'taste' it. These people in turn brought their kin in to the mission. The UAM sent mission Aborigines out with tobacco, food and clothing to meet and encourage incoming groups. The missionaries wanted them to cover their nakedness. The children were rounded up and housed in dormatories while their parents continued to live in camps around the Soak. But many people continued to go on hunting trips back out into the spinifex, to rockholes such as Piling, Puntja, Tjulili, Makeru and the area east of Lake Dey Dey.

Jessie Lennon's own story illustrates well how much people moved around, especially when she was a young woman. Jessie's relations, like the Ooldea people, continued their long-distance ceremonial visits on foot, with camels and by train, throughout the years leading up to and following the Maralinga tests. As she says, Aboriginal people travelled officially and unofficially in open wagons on the railway line: 'we were stealing the train' as one man recalled. From Ooldea, people 'stole' the train west to Kalgoorlie and east to Tarcoola, then walked north. All this was of great concern to the patrol officer who was based at the Woomera rocket range, Walter MacDougall, whose job it was to monitor and prevent Aboriginal movements for safety reasons (there is a photograph of MacDougall on p.129). MacDougall was not a little surprised at the persistence of this level of mobility. In August 1951, he reported that people still travelled between the Musgrave Ranges and Ooldea, and in the region east of the Warburton Ranges. In January 1952, he noted one hundred Ooldea people at Coober Pedy and spoke to three different groups who had travelled between the Musgraves and Ooldea. He reported that this north-south traffic 'could cause concern' to the Woomera authorities. Jessie frequently mentions Lake Phillipson (Pirinya) in her story, how important it was for *inma* (ceremony) and how plentiful the kangaroos, emus and birds were after rain. Lake Phillipson was another place that MacDougall worried about because it was visited by so many people; Lake Phillipson lies southwest of Coober Pedy and was inside 'Zone 1' of the Woomera rocket range danger zone. Once the atomic testing program started in 1953, MacDougall was even more anxious about the many reports of Aboriginal people travelling for ceremonies to Lake Phillipson and on to Coober Pedy.

Closing Ooldea

The most effective way to interrupt the movement of Aboriginal people was to cut their rations, and MacDougall used this technique to good effect. In July 1950, before the atomic tests were even planned for the area, MacDougall recommended that ration depots at Mabel Creek, Mt Clarence, Bulgunnia and Ooldea should be closed down as a way of discouraging Aboriginal movements towards the Woomera area. When in 1950 there was a plan for Ooldea Mission to be relocated further south, MacDougall strongly supported it. For many years there had been proposals for the mission to move; Ooldea was impractical because of the constant threat from encroaching sand dunes, the heat and dust. In the end the mission was closed suddenly in June 1952, surprising everyone even though a move had been likely for several years. It closed because of a dispute within the organisation of the UAM itself, between its federal and state bodies. Harrie Green and his co-workers left at short notice from Ooldea, with Green telling the large gathering of Aboriginal people that they were free to return to their homelands in the north and west. He asked people to divide themselves into groups to go in different directions, and threw open the ration stores. It was a traumatic experience for everyone, and Aboriginal people remembered wailing and crying, not understanding what had happened. Lutheran missionaries from Koonibba, near Ceduna to the south, had been asked to take charge of the situation and to truck people to a temporary camp on the Yalata pastoral property, on the edge of the Nullarbor. This was not familiar country to the desert people, and well over one hundred people 'voted with their feet' and opted to return to traditional country in the north and northwest. One party set off for Kalgoorlie and another party, the Pitjantjatjara, took the train east to Tarcoola from where they began to walk north to Bulgunnia station. Very few people willingly got onto the Lutheran trucks heading south to 'Ooldea Tank' (Monburu) on the new property. As noted in Jessie's book, a few days after this Patrol Officer Walter MacDougall intercepted the Pitjantjatjara group that was headed north, and turned them back. They too unwillingly ended up on the Yalata property, south. MacDougall's employer, the Long Range Weapons Establishment, was very pleased with this 'highly satisfactory' solution to the problems presented by these mobile and unpredictable Aborigines.

There are different memories of this sequence of events, and some observers have jumped to the conclusion that the impending atomic tests were the cause of Ooldea's closure. After all, the public announcement of future tests somewhere in Australia was made in February 1952, only months earlier. However it was a year after the mission closed that a permanent inland test site was recommended by the British, and Maralinga itself was not 'discovered' until October 1953, as already mentioned. Although the atomic testing program was not the cause of the closure of Ooldea Mission, in the end the absence of the mission suited the authorities nicely. It dealt with a place that had been a major drawcard for desert people whose movements through the area would have posed a threat to the testing program. The scientists were relieved that the UAM at Ooldea had already closed down. On 20 October 1953, as he agreed that 'Maralinga' would become the atomic testing site, the Chief Scientist, W.A.S. Butement was recorded as saying,

> There was a mission at Ooldea, or just a little north of Ooldea, but this has now been abandoned, and I am given to understand that this area is no longer used for Aborigines. There was a track from Ooldea up to the north

> *through the area roughly where Emu now is, and further north, but here again I understand that this is now not used, except by one or two elderly blacks and then on rare occasions, and that there is no need whatever for aborigines to use any part of this country around the proposed area.*[6]

What the scientists did not fully understand was just how mobile Aboriginal people still were at that time and that there were considerably more than 'one or two elderly blacks' still walking through the desert. They did not consider how difficult it would be to contact those Aboriginal people who were in the area and warn them about the bomb testing that was soon to start. Later, MacDougall used traditional beliefs in *mamu* (malevolent spirits) to warn people away from the prohibited area.

Fears for the land

When the first of the Maralinga tests took place, most ex-Ooldea people were at Yalata. They reported hearing one or more bombs, seeing smoke; many were frightened that the smoke would come their way and kill them. Some older men thought the soldiers must be preparing for a war. Stories were passed around about poison, *mamu*, bombs, landrovers, soldiers, people disappearing and the *wanampi* (rainbow serpent). On 14 May 1957, four Aborigines of the Milpuddie family were found in the prohibited area near the Marcoo test site: an elderly man, his wife and two children, who had been on the move for 12 months, walking from the Ernabella region to meet relatives at Ooldea.[7] They had walked at least one mile across contaminated land, were found to be contaminated, were forcibly showered by service personnel and transported promptly to Middle Yard camp at what was then known as Tallowan (Yalata). Twenty five years later in 1982, when the ex-Ooldea people first moved back onto the land to form an outstation near Lake Dey Dey (now known as Oak Valley and which is not in a contaminated area), they were still concerned about the 'poison' from the bomb. People worried that the hot summers would draw the poison out of the sand, they were fearful of the effects of the bombs saying they had 'stirred up' the country and made it 'no good'. *Kapi* (rockholes) in the prohibited area such as Talyiri, Piling and Wiluna were thought to be 'finished' and their water not to be trusted.

Agitation

In April 1980, the *Adelaide Advertiser* published a series of articles on the atomic tests and the possible health consequences to individuals who worked at the site. There was a report of the 1957 incident involving the Milpuddies and another about the Black Mist incident. The 'Black Mist' refers to the fallout from the Totem 1 test at Emu on 15 October 1953, which fell on

Yankunytjatjara people at Wallatinna Station, 170 kilometres from the Emu test site, and the surrounding area.[8] The sticky, black dust was said to have caused rashes, vomiting, diarrhoea. It was said that many children became blind and that the old and frail began to die. This is the test that Jessie Lennon talks about in her chapter 'The bomb caught us'.

As a result of the newspaper stories, the extraordinary lack of any official health or environmental follow-up to the tests was exposed to public attention. The South Australian Health Commission hurriedly attempted to examine any disease trends linked with radiation among remote Aboriginal communities, and in February 1981, concluded that inadequate counts of the population and the poor medical records made such research very difficult.[9] By this time many Aboriginal groups and their representative organisations were lobbying for a full investigation. Dr Trevor Cutter from Congress in Alice Springs, Daniel Vachon and Phillip Toyne from the Pitjantjatjara Council, and in 1983 Yami Lester, an Aboriginal man from Wallatinna who went blind, lodged a claim for damages against the Commonwealth.[10] Further claims were proposed.

A Royal Commission into British Nuclear Tests in Australia was eventually set up in July 1984, commenced hearings in August and concluded with final submissions in September 1985.[11] Jessie Lennon and others at Coober Pedy say they were not told about the Royal Commission meetings. Apart from the capital cities, hearings of the Royal Commission were held in April 1985 at Marla Bore, Wallatinna Homestead and a camp near Maralinga. These hearings enabled Aboriginal people to speak out in informal and culturally comfortable settings mostly on their own land, although Cundeelee people from Western Australia travelled to Maralinga to give their evidence.[12] At Wallatinna, Yami Lester and his parents, Eileen Brown (who Jessie mentions several times in her story), and others gave evidence about their experiences of the Black Mist, *puyu* (smoke).[13] As historian Heather Goodall points out, the hearings provided a platform for Aboriginal people to tell the world about the neglect and criminal disregard of their interests by the Australian and British authorities in the 1950s.[14] But lawyers representing Aboriginal groups could not make any definite finding about the Black Mist because of the absence of medical records, the difficulties of relating the fallout to specific health effects, and the lack of scientific knowledge about exposure to low level radiation and the immune system. It was difficult at times to find any reconciliation between the individual or community memories of thirty years before, and the legal and scientific requirements of a Royal Commission.[15]

The Royal Commission heard that the safety of Aborigines was grossly compromised during the tests and that the scientists underestimated the extent of Aboriginal movements through the prohibited area. This was despite reports from patrol officers during the tests that, 'Aborigines had been living well inside the Maralinga Prohibited Zone continuously from before the establishment of the Atomic Weapons Testing Grounds.'[16] When the health physicists had done their calculations of the risks, they had no idea of Aboriginal lifestyle, types of clothing, methods of cooking and food preparation, nor that people were barefoot and slept on the ground.

As a result of the Royal Commission, a compensation package was designed for those who had interests in and attachment to the Maralinga lands — to make it possible to live there. The compensation was made into a trust fund to be used for the lands rather than for individuals: to support infrastructure, for airstrips, the search for drinkable water, and to establish the Oak Valley community there. This was a deliberate decision to avoid unnecessary disputes. Archie Barton, the administrator of the land-holding body Maralinga Tjarutja[17] between 1985 and 2005, led the campaign to rehabilitate and clean up the contaminated land, as recommended by the Royal Commission. After the Royal Commission, a Technical Assessment Group of scientists was created to report on options for different levels of cleanup. The cleanup had to be good enough to allow for Aboriginal people in the future to move back onto the lands and live freely using bush foods.[18] Among other findings, the technical studies discovered that the so-called 'minor' trials had left four major tracts of land contaminated by plutonium: lumps of metal and other debris, tiny fragments, and fine particles small enough to be breathed in.[19] All but some small areas of the Maralinga area were cleared of contaminated material between 1995 and 2000 (a huge and expensive task), althought not everyone agreed that this was the case;[20] the Commonwealth has committed to periodic radiological monitoring. The area known as Section 400 (which includes the Maralinga village site and 3000 remaining square kilometres of land) was handed back to Maralinga Tjarutja in December 2009.[21] There are proposals to establish a museum and eco- and 'nuclear tourism' there as business opportunities for Aboriginal people.

However, the story may not be over yet. In 2010, a new class action against the British government was announced, with Indigenous and non-Indigenous civilians claiming compensation for deaths, illness and miscarriages associated with the tests.[23] Whether they will be able to have any more success than the Royal Commission remains to be seen. A British legal firm has interviewed claimants in conjunction with the Aboriginal Legal Rights Movement (ALRM) in South Australia, but to date the South Australian government has declined to provide funds to support the investigations.[24]

Although Aboriginal people living at Oak Valley on the Maralinga Lands have achieved some kind of resolution in the aftermath of the British nuclear testing program, Jessie Lennon, her family and others from the Coober Pedy region are still afflicted by a sense of grievance, personal pain and loss of voice. They believe the authorities failed to take notice of their stories of the bombs, their experience of the 'smoke' and the ailments they attribute to the radioactivity to which they may well have been exposed. This perceived injustice, together with the anxiety of raised expectations associated with yet another legal investigation, are examples of the continuing and painful legacy of Maralinga for Aboriginal people.

Acknowledgements

I undertook anthropological and health research at Yalata between 1978 and 1982. Kingsley Palmer and I conducted original research in 1984–5 with Yalata and Oak Valley people for the Maralinga hearings of the Royal Commission into British Nuclear Tests in Australia, and for the final submission compiled by Geoff Eames and Andrew Collett. Other contributors to the submission included Chris Clarke, Heather Goodall, David Hope and Daniel Vachon. Kingsley Palmer and I were commissioned by Maralinga Tjarutja between 1987–1989 to document the diet, hunting ranges, dust loadings and lifestyle of Oak Valley residents, as part of the Department of Resources and Energy Technical Assessment Group 'cleanup' studies.

Notes

1. In 1946, the Australian government announced a joint venture with the British government to set up a range for the testing of guided missiles in outback South Australia ('The Long Range Weapons Project.' Statements by Minister for Defence, Commonwealth of Australia, on 22 November 1946 and 10 March 1947). In 1951, there were persistent rumours in Washington USA, that atomic tests would be staged at Woomera because of Britain's existing involvement there.
2. C. Duguid (1947) The Rocket Range, Aborigines and War, Address at the Melbourne Town Hall, 31 March 1947, Rocket Range Protest Committee, Melbourne.
3. P. Toyne and D. Vachon (1984) *Growing up the country. The Pitjantjatjara struggle for their land*, McPhee Gribble/Penguin Books, Melbourne.
4. J.L. Symonds (1985) *A history of British Atomic Tests in Australia*, Department of Resources and Energy, AGPS, Canberra:228.
5. T. Gara, S. Colley, S. Brockwell, S. Cane (1988) *The Aboriginal Metropolis of Ooldea*, A report to Aboriginal Heritage Branch, Department of Environment and Planning, S.A.
6. Cited in J.L. Symonds (1985) *A history of British Atomic Tests in Australia*, Department of Resources and Energy, AGPS, Canberra:256.
7. J.L. Symonds (1985) *A history of British Atomic Tests in Australia*, Department of Resources and Energy, AGPS, Canberra:430–432; see also G.M. Eames and A.C. Collett (1985) *Final Submission by Counsel on behalf of Aboriginal Organisations and Individuals*, Royal Commission into British Nuclear Tests in Australia, 16 September 1985.
8. Robert Ball and Peter de Ionno 'A-Test "mist" may have killed 50', *The Advertiser,* 12 May 1980; 'A "black mist" that brought death', *The Advertiser,* 3 May 1980.

9. 'SA wants check on Aboriginals', *The Advertiser*, 5 May 1980; B. Hailstone (1981) 'A-tests, illness link doubted', *Adelaide Advertiser*, 28 March 1981; Aboriginal Health Unit (1981) *A survey of diseases that may be related to radiation among Pitjantjatjara on remote reserves*, Adelaide, SA Health Commission.
10. 'Aboriginal sues over Emu Field A-blasts', *The Advertiser*, 5–6 February 1983.
11. For a readable account see R. Milliken (1986) *No Conceivable Injury. The story of Britain and Australia's atomic cover-up*, Penguin, Melbourne.
12. Aboriginal people were represented by barristers Geoff Eames and Andrew Collett.
13. G.M. Eames and A.C. Collett (1985) *Final Submission by Counsel on behalf of Aboriginal Organisations and Individuals*, Royal Commission into British Nuclear Tests in Australia, 16 September 1985:138–146.
14. H. Goodall (1992) 'The whole truth and nothing but…' Some intersections of Western Law, Aboriginal history and community memory, *Journal of Australian Studies* 16(35):104–119.
15. Heather Goodall discusses these issues in 'The whole truth and nothing but…'
16. G.M. Eames and A.C. Collett (1985) *Final Submission*:304.
17. Maralinga Tjarutja means 'from down there at Maralinga'. It is a 'new' name.
18. Technical Assessment Group (1990) *Rehabilitation of Former Nuclear Test Sites in Australia*, Department of Primary Industries and Energy, Canberra, AGPS; K. Palmer and M. Brady (1991) *Diet and Dust in the Desert, An Aboriginal community Maralinga Lands, South Australia*, Institute Report Series, AIATSIS, Canberra.
19. P.A. Burns, M.B. Cooper, K.H. Lokan, M.J. Wilks, G.A. Williams (1995) Characteristics of plutonium and americium contamination at the former U.K. Atomic Weapons Test Ranges at Maralinga and Emu, *Appl.Radiat.Isot.* 46(11):1099–1107.
20. A. Parkinson (2007) *Maralinga. Australia's Nuclear Waste Cover-up*, Sydney, ABC Books.
21. Minister for Resources and Energy, Minister for Tourism, 17 November 2009, Press Release: 'Minister signs Maralinga handback deed'.
22. A. McQuire (2010) 'Aboriginal victims to sue British over nuclear tests', *National Indigenous Times*, 194(9).
23. On 22 November 2010, the UK Court of Appeal rejected all but one claimant in a test case mounted by ex-servicemen for nuclear test-related damages against the UK Ministry of Defence.

Timeline

For tens of thousands of years, Aboriginal people walked the land of the Western Desert of Australia which includes the area now known as Coober Pedy.

1858	John McDouall Stuart becomes the first white man to pass through the area.
c.1850s	Some land is settled to the north and west of Port Augusta.
1877	Pastoral lease of Wilgena Station area is issued to T. Hogarth and J. Warren.
by 1885	South Australia Lands and Survey have divided up the entire area into pastoral leases and leases have been issued but not necessarily taken up.
c.1885	Leasees of established pastoral leases of northern South Australia have begun erecting their own dog fences to keep dingoes away from the sheep.
late 1800s	Jessie Lennon's father, Nylatu, is born near Iltur in the far north-west of South Australia.
1896	Leases of the area now known as Granite Downs are taken out by J.J. Anderson.
1900	Wilgena Station is serviced by mail coach.
1902	Gold rush at Tarcoola.
1906	Pastoral lease of area now known as Granite Downs is issued to J.M. Lennon, L.J. Lennon and G.W. Waye.
1912	Construction begins on the East–West (Transcontinental) railway line. Anangu (Aboriginal people) walking the country begin to 'run into the line'.
1915	Will Hutchison becomes the first white person to discover opal in the region.
1915–60	All handwork mining of opal.
1916	'Company's Patch', five kilometres south-west of the present Coober Pedy, becomes the first opal mine of the area.
1916	'The Big Flat' opal field becomes the main field.
1917	East–West (Transcontinental) rail line is completed.
1919	Daisy Bates takes up camp near the line between Ooldea Siding and Ooldea Soak — long a gathering place for the peoples of the Western Desert and others.

1920	The Progress Association of what has become known as Stuart Range votes to change the name of the settlement to Coober Pedy.
1921	Building of the Coober Pedy water tank ensures a more stable water supply.
c.1926	Jessie, daughter of Nylatu and Kutin, is born at Wilgena Station, near Kingoonya.
1930s	Jacob Santing's mail run, a weekly 800 kilometre round trip, becomes Coober Pedy's contact with the outside world.
c.1933	Nylatu takes daughter Jessie with him on a journey to Ooldea, then later on another journey with the Old People to Lake Phillipson, and so into Coober Pedy.
1937	Umeewarra Mission officially begins in Port Augusta.
1939–45	World War II. Jessie lives in Coober Pedy, Kingoonya and at Bon Bon Station.
1945	Jessie Austin and Barney Lennon marry in Port Augusta.
1946	Tottie Bryant discovers opal at Eight Mile leading to a new rush for opal.
1946	Bernard Lennon is born at Eight Mile Field.
1949	Emily Lennon is born at Kingoonya (March).
1949	Beaver Lennon is born in Port Augusta (November).
1950s	Bulldozers, open cut method of opal mining begins at Coober Pedy fields.
1952	Stanley Lennon is born at Eleven Mile Field.
1953	Bombs detonated at Emu Junction, north-west of Coober Pedy. Lennon family flees to Port Augusta (October).
1953	Billy Luke Lennon is born in Port Augusta (November).
1956	Joseph Lennon is born in Port Augusta.
1956–63	Seven further bomb explosions at Maralinga to the south-west, followed by secret, so-called 'minor trials' which involve plutonium.
1959	Aboriginal Reserve is established on the edge of Coober Pedy.
1960s	Waves of immigrant European workers arrive at the opal fields.
1960	Coober Pedy's first school opens.
1962	Judy Strangways is born in Port Augusta.
1964	Clem Michael Lennon is born in Ceduna.
1970s	Jessie Lennon returns to Coober Pedy to live.
1975	The Aboriginal Reserve at Coober Pedy becomes Umoona Community.
1980	Coober Pedy becomes the largest producer of opal in the world.
1982	The sealed and straightened Stuart Highway bypasses Kingoonya.

	Kingoonya Hotel closes, Glendambo Hotel, on the new highway, opens.
1985	The Royal Commission into British Nuclear Testing in Australia begins its hearings.
1987	The new Stuart Highway is completed. Tourism booms in Coober Pedy.
1992–96	Three senior members of the Aboriginal community in Coober Pedy — Jessie Lennon, her husband Ricky Brown, and Larry Crombie — lead a campaign, to date unsuccessful, for compensation from the fallout from the British nuclear testing.
1993	Jessie Lennon initiates work on the book she wants to write 'to leave something for my children, grandchildren and great-grandchildren'.
1993	Expedition with the Wilderness Society of Australia to Jessie's mother, Kutin's homelands at Tjalyiri (Tallaringa).
1994	After negotiations, Mabel Creek Station lease passes to the descendants of Kutin (Rosie Austin), of whom Willie Austin and Jessie Lennon are the senior members.
1996	And I Always Been Moving! the early life of Jessie Lennon is launched in Coober Pedy to family and friends and later at the Adelaide Fringe Festival.
1998	Jessie Lennon passed away (November).
2000	Publication of *I'm the one that know this country!* after many years in production.
2009	Inclusion of an extract from *And I Always Been Moving* with Jessie's biography in the newly published *Macquarie PEN Anthology of Aboriginal Literature*. This was later included in the *Macquarie PEN Anthology of Australian Literature*, published in 2010.

References

Personal communications

H.B. (name under taboo), Yalata, 1992.
Steve Baines, Mayor and Postmaster, Coober Pedy, 2010 (re population).
Michael Balharry, Dog Fence Board, 14 April 1998.
Barka Bryant, Yalata, 1991, 1992.
Ricky Brown, Coober Pedy, 1994.
Alice Mangkatinna Cox, Yalata, 1994.
Eileen Unkari Crombie, Eileen Kampakuta Brown and other members of Kupa Piti Kungka Tjuta, Coober Pedy, 1993–99.
Martha Edwards, Edna Tjantjingu Williams and others, Yalata and Coober Pedy, 1990s.
Joe Kennedy, Adelaide, 1998.
Jessie Lennon, Edna Williams, Eileen Wingfield, Ricky Brown, Larry Crombie and families and others, Coober Pedy, 1993, 1994, 1995, 1996. Meetings re Emu/Maralinga.
Jessie Lennon, Coober Pedy and Whyalla, 1993, 1997.
Jack May and others, Yalata, 1990–92.
Ivy McWilliams, Cowell, 1998.
Merner Muellar, Adelaide, 1998.
Tracey Pierce, Tarcoola, 1998.
Frank Quigley, Adelaide, 2000.
Mick Sincock, Department of Administration and Information Services, South Australia Land Services Group, 21 December 1999.
Myra Tjunmutju Watson, Coober Pedy, 2000.
Tilly Waye, Coober Pedy, 1998.
Tommy Willis, Coober Pedy, 1998 and Port Augusta, 1999.
Bert and Jill Wilson, Coober Pedy, 2000.
Eileen Wani Wingfield, Coober Pedy, 1996, 1998, 1999.
Charlie Jackson, Director of Pika Wiya Health Service, Port Augusta, 2010 (re population).

Bibliography

Adelaide Advertiser, 1958, 1984, 1985.
Andamooka Primary School, *Andamooka: A Short History*, Andamooka, South Australia.
The Atomic Weapons Test Safety Committee 1957, *Report to the Prime Minister on the Buffalo Trials, Maralinga 1956*, Commonwealth of Australia, Melbourne.

References

Australian Bureau of Statistics 2010, *National Regional Profile, Port Augusta 2004–2008*, cat. no. 1379.0.55.001, ABS, Canberra.

Barnes, L.C., Townsend, I.J., Robertson, R.S. & Scott, D.C. 1992, *Opal, South Australia's gemstone*, Department of Mines and Energy, Geological Survey of South Australia, Handbook No. 5.

Bates, Daisy 1938, *The Passing of the Aborigines*, John Murray, London.

Beadell, Len 1967, *Blast the Bush*, Rigby, Adelaide.

Berkery, Frank 1944, *East Goes West*, Fraser & Jenkinson, Melbourne.

Bolam, A.G. 1930, *The Trans-Australian Wonderland*, Barker & Company, Melbourne.

Brady, Maggie 1986, 'Leaving the Spinifex: the impact of rations, missions and the atomic tests on the southern Pitjantjatjara', *Records of the South Australian Museum*, 20: 35–45.

Calder, W. (ed.) 1993, *Telegraph Tourists: Crossing Australia with 'Vauxie' and 'Baby' in 1929*, Jimaringle Publications, Mount Martha.

Caterer, Helen 1981, *Australian Outback: 60 years of Bush Church Aid*, Anglican Information Office, Sydney.

Collett, A. 1985, *ALRM Submission to 'The Report of the Royal Commission into British Nuclear Tests in Australia'*, Australian Government Publishing Service, Canberra.

Cox, Alice Mangkatinna et al. 1994, *Aboriginal Women's Calendar, Yalata/Oak Valley, 1995*, Yalata/Oak Valley, Minyma Tjuṯa, Adelaide.

Crilly, K. 1990, *The Discovery of Coober Pedy*, Coober Pedy Historical Society, Norwood.

Downs, Jim & Dawms, Berthold 1996, *Australia by Rail: The Ghan from Adelaide to Alice*, Lichtbild, Pty. Ltd., Cromer.

Downing, Jim 1988, *Country of My Spirit*, North Australian Research Unit, Darwin.

Faull, Jim 1988, *Life on the Edge*, D.C. of Murat Bay, Ceduna.

Gerard, A.E. 1943, *United Aborigines Mission (of Australia): An outline of the history of the Mission, particularly in South Australia*, UAM, Adelaide.

Goddard, Cliff (comp.) 1992, *Pitjantjatjara/Yankunytjatjara to English Dictionary*, 2nd edition, Institute for Aboriginal Development, Alice Springs.

Green, Harry c.1936–1952, unpublished journals, Ooldea, held at AIATSIS, Canberra.

Hall, Frank c.1940s, Sand, Spinifex and Smiling Faces, unpublished manuscript, held at AIATSIS, Canberra.

Holden, Philip 1991, *Along the Dingo Fence,* Hodder & Stoughton, Sydney.

Johnson, Anne 2006, *Digging around Cooper Pedy: exploring life in the little opal mining town with a big profile*, Sandstone Press, Coober Pedy.

Jones, Max 1989, *Tracks*, Stewart Maxwell Jones, Renmark.

Leechman, F. 1968, *The Opal Book*, Ure Smith, Sydney.

Lester, Yami 1997, radio interview, ABC.

Mattingley, Christobel & Hampton, Ken (eds) 1988, *Survival In Our Own Land*, Wakefield Press, Adelaide.

McClelland, James et al. 1985, *The Report of the Royal Commission into British Nuclear Tests in Australia*, Australian Government Publishing Service, Canberra.

Medway, K.E. 1980, *Coober Pedy: 65 Years Young 1915–1980*, K.E. Medway, Norwood.

Miles, B. 1954, *The Stars My Blanket*, John Murray, London.

The Nuclear Issues Coalition 1997, *The Economic Impact of Mining at Roxby Downs*, Conservation Council, Adelaide.

Olympic Dam Project Committee 1982, *The Olympic Dam Project*, Western Mining & B.P. Australia, Melbourne.

Rees, C. & Rees, L. 1971, *Australia: The Big Sky Country*, Ure Smith, Sydney.

Ryan, T. c.1980, Recollections as a Coober Pedy miner in 1930, unpublished manuscript.

Skewes, Janet (comp.) 1997, *Coober Pedylanguru Tjukurpa: stories from Anangu of Coober Pedy*, Umoona Community Council, Coober Pedy.

Turner, M. 1960s, 'Central Australian Railway', in *The Ghan*, Marree School, Marree.

Turner, Violet E. 1950, *Ooldea*, S. John Bacon, Melbourne.

Wake, P.V. 1969, *Opal Men*, Reed, Sydney.

Westney, Candida & Percival, Dinah 1989, *Fence People*, Hutchinson Australia, Milsons Point.

Woods, Kim (comp.) 1988, *Tarcoola: A Small History and Trail Guide*, Tarcoola Area School, Tarcoola.